The Book Palace
Jubilee House
Bedwardine Road
Crystal Palace
London SE19 3AP

Email: info@illustratorsmag.com
Web: www.illustratorsmag.com
Tel: 020 8768 0022
(from overseas +44 20 8768 0022)

Publisher: Geoff West
Editor & Designer: Peter Richardson
Consultant Editors: Bryn Havord, David Ashford
and David Roach
Online Editor: Paul Tanner
Featured Writers: David Ashford, David Roach

For advertising information, rates and
specifications, please contact Geoff West at the
address above or at: **illustratorsmag.com**
illustrators (ISBN 978-1-907081-17-0)
Issue Number One Summer 2012
Copyright © 2012 by The Book Palace Ltd

illustrators is published quarterly.
Four Issue Subscriptions:
£55 post free UK
£77 airmail Europe
£89 airmail USA/ rest of world

Cover Image: Denis McLoughlin's cover for Jack
Dolph's Hot Tip TVB 145, published March 1954.

Printed in China by Prolong Presss Ltd

ISSUE ONE, VOLUME ONE SUMMER 2012

CONTENTS

EDITORIAL

Welcome to the first issue of **illustrators,** a journal devoted to celebrating the often-unsung talents of British and European illustrators. We intend to create in this and successive issues a lasting reference library of articles written and designed with passion and dedication, bringing you some of the most exciting art the printed page has ever seen.

illustrators is very much a team effort and the issue that you hold in your hands would never have happened had it not been for the generosity and assistance provided by our consulting editors David Roach and David Ashford as well as invaluable advice and input from Bryn Havord and Rian Hughes.

Thanks also to Mrs. Janet Mason, Roger Peacey, Steve Taylor, Jeremy Briggs, Phil Rushton, Richard Burton and Mark Terry of Facsimile Dust Jackets L.L.C (www.facsimiledustjackets.com). Our special thanks to Calum Laird and Bill McLoughlin at DC Thomson, who generously granted us permission to reproduce so much of Ian Kennedy's stellar artwork as well as the photograph of Ian in his studio.

We hope that our journal will inspire readers with our own deep enthusiasm and delight in the captivating art of illustration.

Denis and Dorothy ham it up for the cover of Sam Ross's *Tight Corner*.
Published in 1957, it was numbered 158 out of over five hundred covers
that McLoughlin produced for the *American Bloodhound Mystery* series.

Dames, Guns and Danger

The Hardboiled Art of Denis McLoughlin

A personal reminiscence by David Ashford

I FIRST CAME across the hard-boiled art of Denis McLoughlin in the orange/green comics that were on sale in the large Woolworth store in my home town of Torquay in South Devon. I would have been about seven or eight years old. Not that I would have used the term "hard-boiled" then but I certainly thought that here was an artist whose drawings were plenty tough. I knew his name right off, too, because each of the comics' covers was signed "d. mcloughlin", in lower case, which was unusual. These small, twelve page three-penny comics that I found so appealing featured a tough detective or "special agent" called *Roy Carson;* a time traveller, *Swift Morgan* (who looked not unlike a spaceman I had seen in the Saturday matinee serials in our local cinema and who had the rather similar name of *Flash Gordon*) and a favourite of mine from other comics, *Buffalo Bill.* Also in the same comic format was another character called *Blackhawk*, featuring a bunch of American airmen, but this didn't have the same appeal for me - the artist was different. In fact, for a while, the *Buffalo Bill* comics were also disappointing because, for a time, this strikingly tough new artist I had discovered drew only the covers, and the interior work was markedly inferior. I remember being really pleased when, a little later, I found the entire *Buffalo Bill comic* was drawn by "d. mcloughlin".

The first time I saw the *Buffalo Bill Wild West Annual* was in a classroom at my primary school. A classmate had brought in a book he'd just been given for his birthday and, when he showed it me, I was enthralled by it. I just couldn't believe it: all the drawings - and the paintings - were by Denis McLoughlin (I knew his full name now as it was there on the title page). Looking through it, I was thrilled to see that this annual was all about the real, historical West, something about which I knew very little but was very eager to learn. I became absolutely hooked on those annuals and, indeed, anything drawn by Denis McLoughlin. (Strangely enough, it was not until I was in my late twenties that I discovered the many hundreds of wonderful covers he had

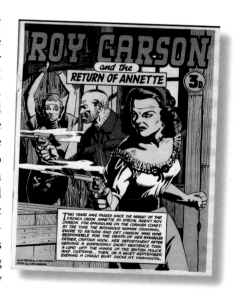

Roy Carson and the Return of Annette,
**TV Boardman Comic No. 34
December 1950.**

done for the Boardman novels and pulp magazines). Those *Buffalo Bill Annuals*, packed full of information on the Old West - the Indians, the scouts, the gunfighters, stagecoaches, old mines, forts, practically every aspect of the West you could possibly think of - fascinated me. And these volumes were all so superbly designed, with so much attention to detail and always with such a feeling of rugged authenticity. I remember thinking as a boy how great it would be to meet this remarkable artist who obviously loved the American West with a passion and knew so much about its history.

It would be a very long time before that wish came true, but come true it did, almost thirty years later. At the first *British Comicon* organised by Denis Gifford in 1976, I met the man himself. We hit it off straight away and a friendship between us began that day that was to last right up until his death in 2002.

My first impression of Denis McLoughlin was how short and slight he was. I had been expecting a big, rather tough-looking guy, similar to the characters in so many of his illustrations and here was this "little fellah" (as he described himself) who couldn't be more than five foot three inches – but then James Cagney was a little guy and he was plenty tough! McLoughlin was very neatly attired in jacket and tie but somehow there was nothing conventional about his dress. Without in any way appearing outrageous, here was a man who was happy to stand out a little from the crowd. He was flattered to hear how much I admired his work and for how long I had held it in such high esteem – since I was eight years old in fact! What a pity it was, he told me, that I had not written to tell him that when I was a boy, but, as I told him, that wasn't something you think of doing when you're a kid. It was obvious that, in a completely unselfconscious way, Denis McLoughlin enjoyed praise

It was something I quickly discovered about Denis; there was no false

ABOVE: *Okay Adventure Annual, 1955. This artwork was also used for the cover of The Ace Adventure Album.*

RIGHT: *Kit Carson Indian Fighter. Colour plate for Buffalo Bill Annual No. 4, published September 1952.*

modesty about him. He knew he was good and he liked people to agree with him! Unfortunately, living in Bolton and working only on children's comics as he was at that time (something that does not automatically confer instant admiration from most members of the public) there were few if any people he could rub shoulders with who could bolster his artistic ego. Obviously he would hear good reports about his artwork from editors via letter or phone but this was not the same as actually meeting, face-to-face, people who found his work so endlessly fascinating. This is certainly not to say that he expected unstinted praise for all his work. He would often describe some early paperback cover of his that I had come across as "lousy". Incidentally, Denis never had an agent for his artwork, "never needed one", he told me – although he was to hire a literary agent later when he worked on his encyclopaedia of the American West, *Wild and Woolly*.

In the years to come, Mac, as he liked his friends to call him, was to become a regular guest at the annual *Paperback Fair* organised by Maurice Flanagan. He would always give me a call first to check whether or not I was going but, once there, he was in his element, chatting to customers and basking in their adulation. At last he felt his work was being really appreciated for its artistic worth. The person most responsible for McLoughlin's work becoming more and more popular in the U.S. is Californian lawyer, Tom Lesser. A fervent admirer of Mac's work, Lesser visited Mac at his Bolton home, bought a large number of Boardman thrillers and came, as he says, "to love the guy".

There was a great deal to love about Mac. Most of all I think I loved his

ABOVE: Endpapers to *Buffalo Bill's True West Annual*, published in 1961. It was the 13th in the series and, although McLoughlin was working on a fourteenth edition, the project was shelved, making this book the last to appear.

ABOVE: The artist in his Breightmeit studio.

FACING PAGE TOP: Endpapers to *Buffalo Bill Annual No.11*, published 1962.

FACING PAGE BOTTOM: Denis McLoughlin strikes a pose as reference for the *Buffalo Bill Annual*.

enthusiasm for life, which was really contagious. He was in his sixties when I got to know him but he was like a kid, always coming up with new enthusiasms but never ridding himself of the old. His favourite word for anything that pleased him was "fabulous". I can never hear that word without thinking of Mac and his lip-smacking intonation. He was never interested in computers and new electronic gadgets but new toys, particularly if they had something to do with the American West, were fascinating to him. He was also interested in new movies and TV film series, again especially if they were connected to his beloved West. He was even interested in the TV

CONTENTS

and radio work I was doing at the time, which, apart from an appearance as Frank James (Jesse's brother) in a radio play, never had anything to do with the West!

There were, however, a few occasions when I found myself appearing on the radio as an authority on the West – and this was all down to my friendship with Denis McLoughlin. His book, *Wild and Woolly*, had just come out and the BBC had contacted him to ask him to appear on a type of phone-in programme as historical consultant on the American West. He turned them down but told them that David Ashford might be interested! Thanks to Mac the BBC believed that I was an expert on the West and I had no intention of disabusing them. Suddenly I found myself live on radio answering, at some length, questions on Sitting Bull, the Wounded Knee Massacre and Buffalo Bill Cody. Like Denis I was a Western enthusiast and certainly knew something about the West (it was thanks to Denis' *Buffalo Bill Annuals* that I had come to love the historical West as much as the Hollywood version) and I'm pleased to say that the programmes went down pretty well.

Being a friend of Mac meant that you would be constantly surprised by the gifts that would suddenly arrive by post, usually without any warning. Apart from his generous gifts of mint *Buffalo Bill Annuals*, he would send 'pulls' of his Boardman crime novel covers (to keep if he had spares, to return if not) and any original drawings he came across that he thought I might like (an unused illustration from a *Buffalo Bill Annual* particularly

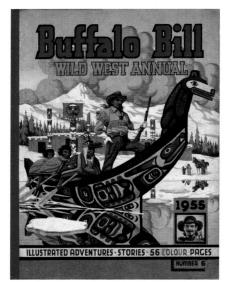

TOP LEFT *Buffalo Bill Wild West Annual No. 6*, dated 1955, published September 1954.

TOP RIGHT: *Buffalo Bill Wild West Annual No. 4*, published September 1952.

BOTTOM LEFT: *Buffalo Bill Wild West Annual No. 2*, published September 1950.

FACING PAGE: McLoughlin's iconic cover for *Buffalo Bill Wild West Annual No. 3*, published September 1951.

delighted me). Knowing my interest in such things, he would send all kinds of items connected with the American West such as a "gen'wine" metal sheriff badge, 'joy house tokens' ("Good for All Night $3 Bath Included") and beautifully designed stitch-on shoulder badges, one denoting the wearer was a United States Marshal, the other identifying him as a member of the Pima County Sheriff's dept. Most of these items had been sent to him by his old army buddy, Bill Bavin, who was then living in Tucson, Pima County, Arizona, having 'earned his pile' in real estate over here. Bavin, a man of large proportions and personality to match, had, according to Mac, "got himself into the Pima County Sheriff's deptartment". Later Bavin became captain of the 'Search and Rescue Posse', which tracked down poor old greenhorns who had wandered off into the desert and got lost. Soon, just as night follows day, through the post came yet another shoulder badge from Mac, this one bearing the legend 'Search and Rescue'.

William S. Bavin meant a great deal to Denis McLoughlin. They had first met during the war when both men were garrisoned at Woolwich. As Mac

Buffalo Bill
WILD WEST ANNUAL

PICTORIAL FEATURES · STORIES · ARTICLES · COLOUR PAGES

The Nobles

THE NOBLES, exclusive and international, dedicated to integrity and adverse to hypocrisy, honour the undermentioned by admission to their Order, in recognition of his/her sharing these convictions.

DAVID ASHFORD

(Signed) William S. Bavin
FRSA, ACIB, FCL
(Founder)

NULLA TAURUS

was "a first class singer and guitar player who appeared in many shows at the garrison theatre. Bill was six foot two inches next to my five foot three inches, was built like a blockhouse and had the largest feet in show business". Mac went to the christening of Bill's "first offspring" and, when Bavin left Woolwich to join the Military Police, "he came back from time to time for a chat". When Bavin decided to found an organisation he called *The Nobles*, it was, of course, to Mac that he turned when he wanted a logo designed. Bill detested what he called 'bull' and membership was limited "to those who can honestly be described as without hypocrisy". The logo depicted a bull's head with a red stripe across it bearing the legend "Nulla Taurus", which was (unfortunately grammatically incorrect) Latin for 'No Bull'!

Again I have Mac to thank for getting me admitted to this 'noble order'. As Bill Bavin wrote: "I have known 'Mac' – Denis McLoughlin – since our army days and have so much respect for his word and judgement that when he recommended you for membership to our association, *The Nobles*, I was prepared to confirm your acceptance without further query". Shortly after receiving Bill Bavin's letter, I happened to go over to California to do a TV commercial set in the Mojave Desert (the nearest I ever got to being in a Western; at least the setting was right although the subject matter certainly wasn't - the launch of a new car!). While I was there I looked up a fellow member of *The Nobles*, Rod Peterson, who happened to be the writer/producer of the long-running, homespun TV series, *The Walton's*. Rod gave me a great time, showing me all over the old Universal Studios exterior sets and even taking photos of me in the deserted streets of the Western town I had seen in so many old movies. That evening he and his charming wife treated

ABOVE: David Ashford's membership card to The Nobles, designed by Denis McLoughlin.

ABOVE RIGHT: McLoughlin's close friend Bill Bavin living the dream in Tucson Arizona.

FACING PAGE: Discarded rough for cover of *Buffalo Bill Annual No. 7.*

ABOVE: Original art for the _Buffalo Bill Wild West Annual No. 11_ endpapers.

FACING PAGE: A rough for _New Frontiers_, a proposed annual that never saw print.

me to my very first Mexican meal in a classy restaurant they frequented. A year or so later I met the artist brother of Mrs Peterson, William Whittaker, when he visited London with his family and we got on really well. He is a superb artist and loves the West as much as Mac and me, although his own artistry tends towards portraiture. Both of these valuable friendships are the direct result of my getting to know Mac. I really owe him so very much.

Knowing all about Mac's fascination for the American West, Bill Bavin tried on so many occasions to get him to go out to Arizona all expenses paid but, try as he might, he just couldn't persuade him to make the trip. When I queried his reason for not wanting to go out there, he replied that he was afraid that the reality wouldn't live up to his vision of the West. This is a fascinating insight into the man and his art. He was someone who lived so much in his imagination. He was a true artist, turning reality into his own romantic vision. The word 'romantic' might seem an odd one to use in connection with Denis McLoughlin's hard-edged art, but it is just as apposite as it is when assessing the work of other Western artists such as the great 19th century American Western illustrators, Frederic Remington and Charlie Russell, both of whom appear to show the West as it really was and are praised for their historical authenticity. It is only when you compare their paintings and drawings with the actual photographs of the period and do some reading of historical accounts that you realise the romanticising that has taken place in their work. In the later _Buffalo Bill Annuals_ when Mac was endeavouring to bring greater historical authenticity to his illustrations, it is possible to discern the difficulty he is having in trying to create images

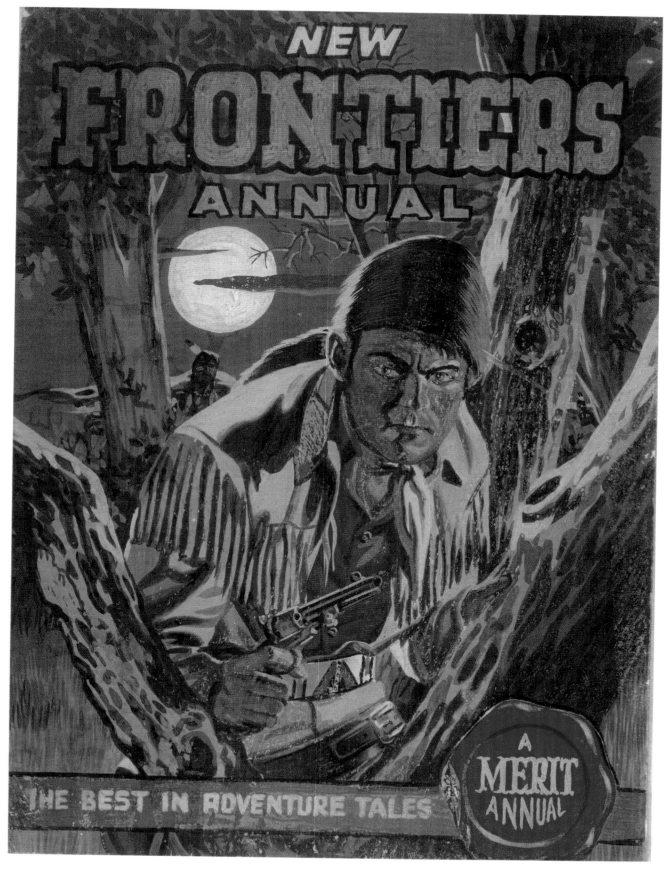

TOP: Envelope design for
McLoughlin's personal stationery.

that are at once reasonably historically accurate and at the same time correspond to the mythology of the West as it would have been understood by the majority of his young readers. He certainly succeeded more than most and Denis McLoughlin's West has a rugged authenticity all it's own. I'm sure I'm not alone in saying, in relation to McLoughlin's work, if the West wasn't like this, it should have been.

One person I knew who did not quite share my opinion of McLoughlin's West was Joan Whitford. Joan was a regular writer on Western subjects for the comics of the Amalgamated Press such as *Knockout* and *Sun* and, under her best-known pen name of Barry Ford, wrote many stories featuring, among others, *Buffalo Bill* and *Wild Bill Hickok*. Her splendid series covering facts and legends of the West, *Barry Ford's Western Scrapbook,* ran for many years in *Sun* and was endlessly reprinted in various picture libraries and annuals. After the departure of writer Arthur Groom from the *Buffalo Bill Annuals*, it was Joan Whitford who was chosen to take over writing the text stories. Under the new nom de plume of Rex James, she brought her own knowledge of the West to the annual and, with it, a certain sense of historical authenticity that was missing from the text stories by Arthur Groom, good storyteller that he was. That is not to say that Joan didn't bring her own romanticism to bear in her writing for the annual: her fictional stories featured Doc Holliday as an unlikely hero. Joan transformed the historical Doc Holliday from a mean, bad-tempered consumptive gambler into a "strikingly handsome" roving, buckskin-clad, frontier doctor who "had no use for law-breakers". What is interesting to me about Joan Whitford as a Western

ABOVE: *The Battle of Adobe Walls* **original art for a double page spread from**
Buffalo Bill Wild West Annual No. 12, **published 1961.**

ABOVE: *Alibi Baby*, American Bloodhound No. 117, published November 1955.

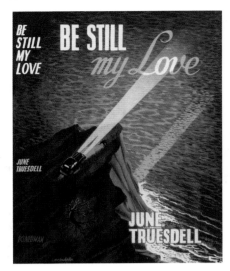

writer is that she had the great good fortune of having her tales illustrated by the very best of British talent, among them: Derek Eyles, Patrick Nicolle, Geoff Campion and Denis McLoughlin. When I asked her who was her favourite illustrator, her prompt, unhesitating answer was "Derek Eyles". When I asked her why she preferred Eyles to McLoughlin her answer was informative: "I loved Eyles' romantic drawing style and his beautiful horses. I wasn't keen on Denis McLoughlin's illustrations as I found them rather brutal". I actually agree with Joan that Derek Eyles' drawings are indeed far more suitable to her softer, more romantic view of the American West than McLoughlin's art. After all, Mac's West was "Wild and Woolly"!

Interestingly, Mac never seemed to be particularly taken with the Hollywood Western. When I used to talk of certain Western films I particularly liked, he was always somewhat non-committal. The only Western that seemed particularly to appeal to him was a rather obscure film directed by Robert

TOP LEFT: *Be Still My Love,* **published by TV Boardman August 1948.**

TOP RIGHT: *Veronica Died Monday,* **Bloodhound Mystery 54, June 1953.**

BOTTOM LEFT: *But Death Runs Faster,* **TVB Paperback 73, 1949.**

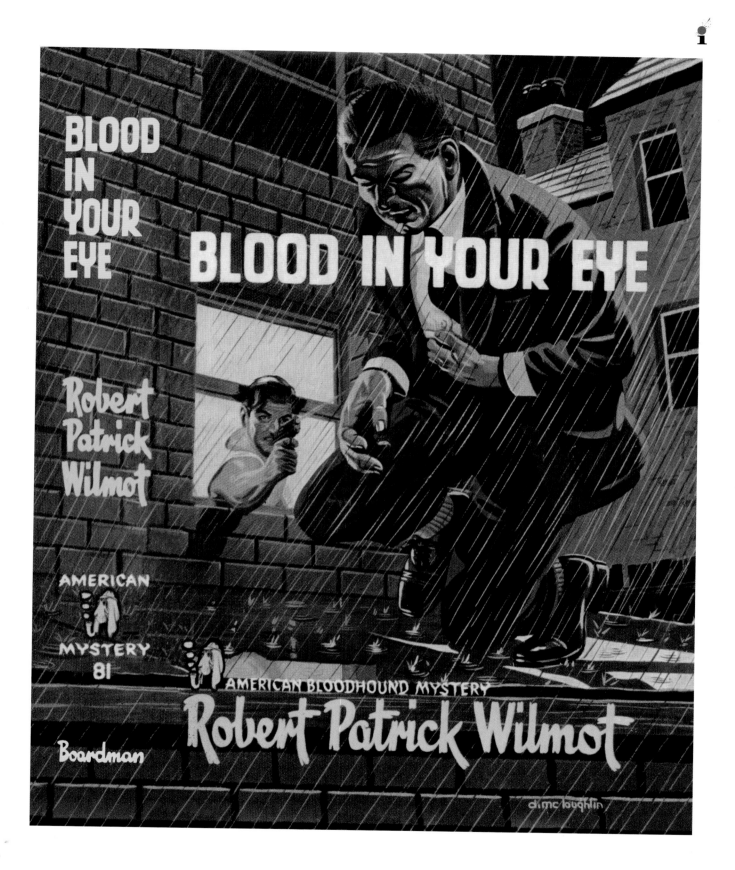

ABOVE: *Blood in Your Eye*, Bloodhound Mystery 81, August 1954.

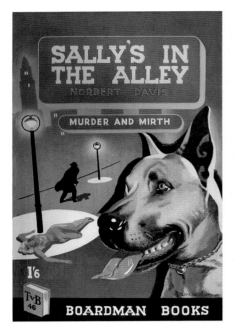

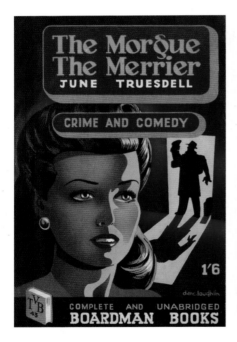

TOP LEFT: *Sally's In The Alley,*
TVB paperback 46, 1947.

TOP RIGHT: *The Corpse On The
Hearth,* TVB paperback 54, 1948.

BOTTOM LEFT: *The Morgue The
Merrier,* TVB paperback 43, 1947.

FACING PAGE: *Wake The Sleeping
Wolf,* Bloodhound Mystery 66,
November 1953.

Altman and starring Warren Beatty and Julie Christie. The film was *McCabe
and Mrs Miller* and Mac lavished praise on it for its rawness and its uncom-
promising lack of romanticism. He loved the primitive quality of the town
the film depicted, the mud, and later in the film, the thick snow covering the
streets. However, there can't be much doubt that he was influenced by the
fluid camera movements of John Ford's classic Westerns. I think particularly
of the marvellous picture strip in the second *Buffalo Bill Annual* entitled *The
Fight.* The strip simply shows a stagecoach being chased by hostile Indians
and it could act as a storyboard for a director to film. This brilliant piece of
visual storytelling must have been influenced by his having seen John Ford's
classic movie, *Stagecoach*, which contains just such a chase. As I once told

Continued on page 22

WAKE THE
Sleeping Wolf

66

A BLOODHOUND MYSTERY BY
Rae Foley

d. mcloughlin

Boardman

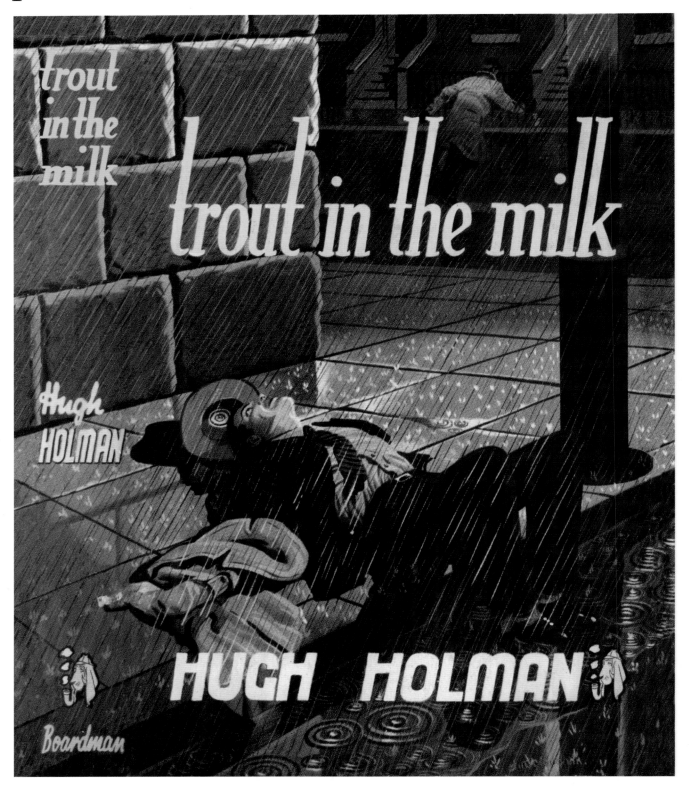

ABOVE: *Trout In The Milk,* Bloodhound Mystery (not numbered but 23rd in the series), August 1951.

FACING PAGE: *Best American Detective Stories of the Year 1951,* first published October 1952.

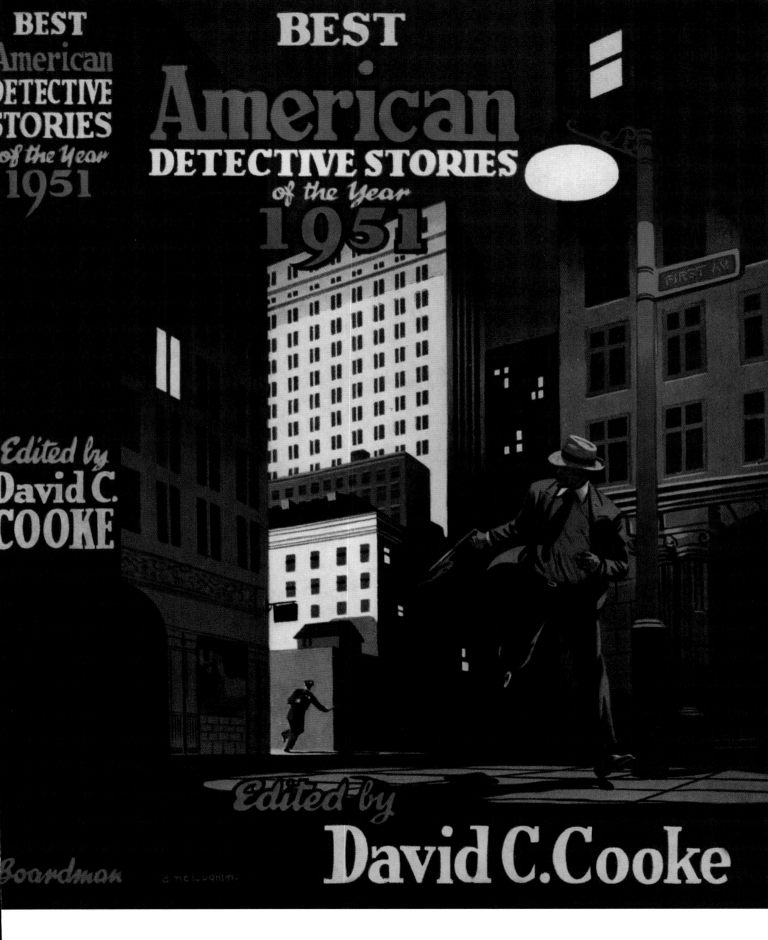

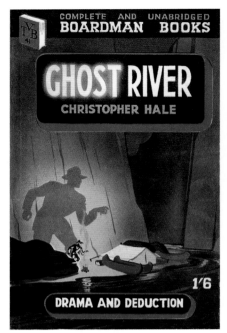

TOP LEFT: *Ghost River*, **TVB paperback 41, 1947.**

TOP RIGHT: *White For A Shroud*, **TVB paperback 71, 1949.**

BOTTOM LEFT: *The Footsteps*, **TVB paperback 68, 1949.**

Mac, he would have made a great Western film director.

And he would have made a great film director of another genre as well. His love of the 'film noir' movies of the forties and early fifties is obvious and their influence is everywhere to be seen in his cover work for the Boardman thrillers, particularly in the paperbacks. Looking today at those early film noirs on TV or on DVD, and knowing McLoughlin's cover work for these novels, it is impossible not to notice the influence. Indeed, sometimes I see a scene in such a film and am taken aback by its similarity to one of Mac's cover paintings. The noir movies were not, of course, the only influences on his cover work. Another major influence was the lurid covers of the American pulp magazines that were on sale in newsagents throughout

ABOVE: McLoughlin strikes a pose with his revolver. Despite reassuring friends and family it was a replica, the gun in fact was all too real.

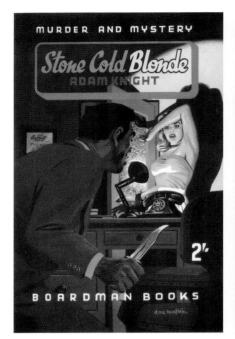

the country just after the War. He was much taken with images of the beautiful dame in dangerous, distressful situations, often with more than a touch of bondage thrown in, which were the staple fare for these covers. He often used this theme in his *Roy Carson* comics, particularly in *Roy Carson and the Return of Annette*, where a shapely female is shown gagged and bound, her arms stretched above her head and tied to some rafters. Ironically, it was this comic that a schoolboy is shown reading in the infamous photograph that appeared in *Picture Post* to illustrate the horrors of American imported comics!

Mac loved pretty much everything about America. It seemed that sometimes, in his imagination, he was actually living in the States. He loved the way Americans spoke and dressed in the movies of the forties and, although he couldn't disguise his strong Bolton accent, there was always a touch of the States in his speech rhythms and certainly in his letter writing. In one letter, asking me whether I would be going to a comic convention, he wrote: "Don't know iffen I'll be able to". He would often use such phrases as "a lotta rubbish" and "someplace" instead of "somewhere", all adding colour to his writing. He was always a stylish dresser, influenced very much by the American movies and remembered 1930's newsreels of Prohibition Chicago

ABOVE: *Stone Cold Blonde*, TVB Paperback 147, published April 1954.

ABOVE RIGHT: McLoughlin's previous take on this subject, *Stone Cold Blonde*, American Bloodhound 37, published May 1952.

FACING PAGE: *The Deep End*, American Bloodhound Mystery 62, published September 1953.

The DEEP END

Fredric Brown

The
DEEP
END

62

Boardman

A BLOODHOUND MYSTERY BY

Fredric Brown

a. mc loughin

NIGHT OF THE JABBERWOCK

Fredric BROWN

A NEW MYSTERY BY

Fredric Brown

Boardman

where everyone wore trilby hats and wide-shouldered overcoats. Photos of him taken in the 1940s show a dapper little guy who could have stepped straight out of a Hollywood film noir. As Raymond Chandler's Phillip Marlowe walked "the mean streets" of L.A. so, in his Roy Carson comics of the late forties, McLoughlin had his hero walking the mean streets of Bolton! The police behave in the *Roy Carson* strips like American cops and even carry tommy guns. In his imagination and in his art he transformed his own environment into a version of America.

The actual real life of Denis McLoughlin could not in fact be more English. Born in Bolton, Lancashire, on 15 April 1918, to Edith and William McLoughlin, he had by his own account an idyllic childhood. His talent for drawing and painting showed itself at an early age and he was constantly winning painting competitions that were organised by several of the local stores. Young Denis was certainly a bright pupil as, despite losing the first two years of schooling through illness, he won a scholarship to the prestigious Whitebank School at the age of eleven and then, at the age of fourteen, won another scholarship to the Bolton School of Art.

The family enjoyed a good standard of living for the time and his father, who was a "hair specialist" ("mornings by appointment only"), made sure that his artistic son had all the best artists' materials available, such as sable brushes and good quality pencils, pens and Indian ink. Both parents encouraged his talent to the full and there seemed to be much love in the

ABOVE: "The Inseparables", Denis (left) and younger brother Colin in their boyhood days.

FACING PAGE: *Night of the Jabberwock, Bloodhound Mystery (not numbered but 27th in series), October 1951.*

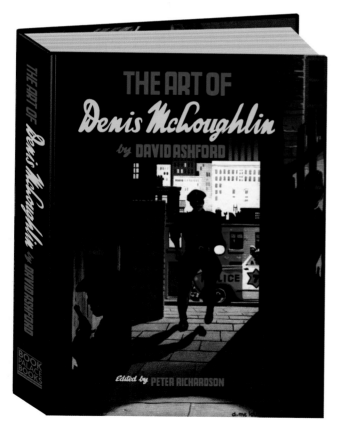

The Art of Denis McLoughlin

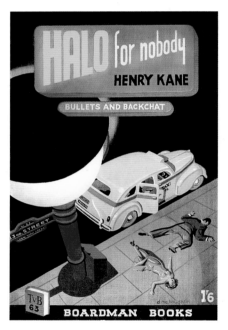

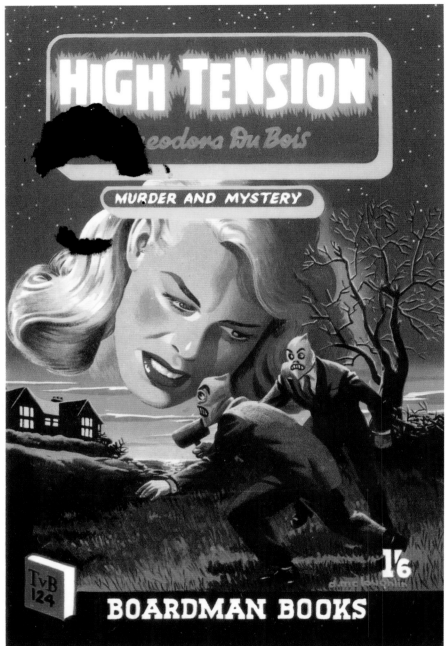

TOP LEFT: *Smokescreen,* TVB paperback 66, 1949.

TOP RIGHT: *High Tension,* TVB paperback 124, April 1953.

BOTTOM LEFT: *Halo For A Nobody,* TVB paperback 63, 1949.

FACING PAGE: *The Cavalier's Corpse,* Bloodhound Mystery 56, July 1953.

family, although it is significant that Mac always called his Mother 'Mother' while his father was always 'Dad'. Although his Mother thought the world of her gifted son, Edith McLoughlin it appears was a fairly domineering personality and was not averse to delivering a little corporal punishment now and again. His Father, on the other hand, was always described by Mac as being "gentle" and quiet" and they had a great relationship.

According to Mac, however, the best thing that happened to him in his childhood was the advent of a younger brother, Colin. He was seven when Colin was born and they immediately formed a bond that was never to be broken. They appear to have had the ideal fraternal relationship. They were constantly together, each one looking out for the other, playing together and

THE
cavalier's
CORPSE

Theodora
DU BOIS

56

A BLOODHOUND MYSTERY BY

Theodora Du Bois

d. mc loughlin

Boardman

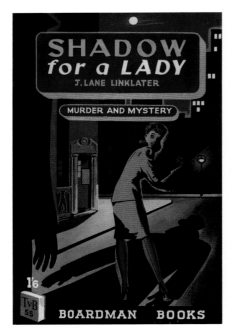

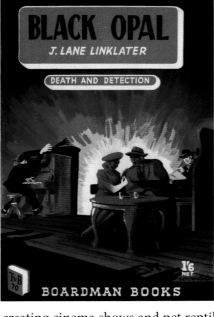

TOP LEFT: *Shadow For A Lady,* **TVB paperback 55, 1948.**

TOP CENTRE: *Black Opal,* **TVB paperback 90, 1949.**

TOP RIGHT: *The Woman Swore Revenge,* **TVB paperback 70, 1951.**

BOTTOM LEFT: *The Devil and Destiny,* **TVB paperback 88, 1949.**

creating cinema shows and pet reptile shows in their back yard (and charging halfpenny admission to the other kids of the neighbourhood!). This close relationship was to continue throughout their adulthood. During the War, when Mac, as a Royal Artillery gunner, was stationed at Woolwich barracks, the brothers would meet up for drinks on their nights off and think up jokes together for the Kangaroo cartoon books. Of course, later, Colin was to write the scripts not only for the majority of the Boardman comics Mac drew but also for all the strips he did in the *Buffalo Bill Annuals*. They became a really strong team. The close relationship between the brothers continued right up until Colin's tragic death in 1988.

Mac was always adamant that there was no sibling rivalry between him and Colin despite the fact that, as he said, "Colin had the looks". Mac was always a puny child, prone to asthma, and must have felt some feelings of physical inadequacy. He certainly was not destined to look like one of his heroes. He was to make up for this, however, by constantly using himself in various guises in illustrations for the *Buffalo Bill Annuals*; in one memorable endpaper painting depicting himself having a gunfight with himself! Later, in his *Commando* work for D.C. Thomson, he would depict himself in the odd panel, never giving himself a major role, only walk-on parts!

Colin McLoughlin may have had the looks but it was his brother who got the girl!! In June 1948 Denis McLoughlin married Dorothy Bain. He had his love for "going to the pictures" to thank for this for he was to meet Dorothy, early in the War, while she was working as a waitress in Bolton's Capitol Cinema Café. Once married they lived together with Mac's parents - and Colin - in Derby Street, Bolton, until, some six or seven years later, they could afford to move into the more prosperous residential area of Bolton called Breightmet. The couple were to remain in their fine, large new house for the rest of their lives. (It's interesting to note that brother Colin remained in the original family home even after the death of their parents, and remained a bachelor all his life.) Mac and Dorothy had a very strong relationship that was to last all their lives. He often used Dorothy as a model and, judging by the photos he took of her in various poses, she obviously enjoyed the work! A marvellous photo of them together

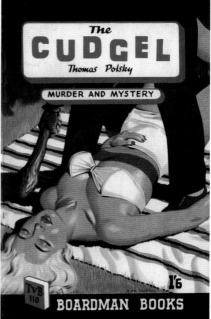

in dramatic pose (see page 2) was used for the cover of Boardman's *Bloodhound Mystery* entitled *The Tight Corner*.

Mac would have been the first to say that he led a pretty charmed life. He had enjoyed a fun-filled childhood; had very supportive parents; a brother whom he adored and with whom he was to share in some of his very best work; a "cushy number" (to use his own words) during the War in which he spent most of his time painting large murals for the Woolwich barracks' canteens; a loving wife who admired and respected his work and loved to help out with any modelling that was required; a fulfilling working life that began in the 1940s and continued right up until his death and a great friend-ship with a man whom he had first met in the Army, Bill Bavin. Unfortu-nately the last years of Mac's life were not to turn out to be nearly as happy

TOP LEFT: *Night Of The Jabberwock,* TVB paperback 125, 1953.

TOP RIGHT: *The Cudgel,* TVB paperback 110, 1952.

BOTTOM RIGHT: *Easy to Murder,* TVB paperback 112, 1952.

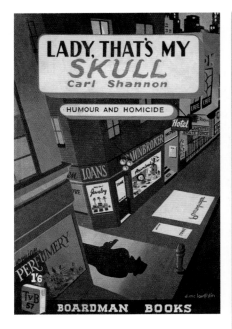

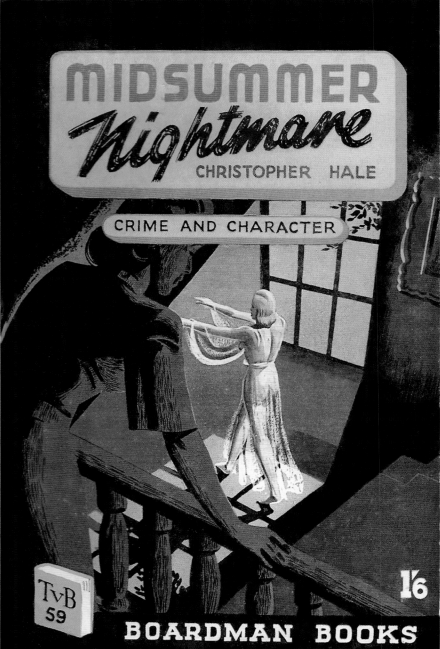

TOP LEFT: *Lady That's My Skull,* TVB paperback 57, 1948.

TOP CENTRE: *Midsummer Nightmare,* TVB paperback 59, 1948.

BOTTOM LEFT: *Cheer For The Dead,* TVB paperback 67, 1949. The artist's brother, Colin McLoughlin, appears in the photo bottom left of cover.

and trouble free.

The storm clouds appeared first in the mid 1980s with the shocking news of the sudden death of Bill Bavin. In the summer of 1985, Bill had been planning to make a visit to England. In fact on the morning of the 8 July I had received a letter from him that he was coming over and that he and his wife would come to see us. That same night, around midnight, I had a distraught call from Mac to say that he had just had Captain Bob Gibson of the Pima County Sheriff's Dept. on the line to tell him that the small plane Bill had been flying had nose-dived and crashed in the desert outside Tucson and that he and his passenger were dead. As if this was not tragedy enough, just over three years later, his brother Colin died. When Colin failed to ar-

ABOVE: *Nirvana Can Also Mean Death*, Boodhound Mystery 283, December 1959.

DETECTIVE TALES

Contents

ABOVE TOP: Banner title for one of Boardman's Popular Press Pulp series, *Private Eye Detective Tales*, published 1952.

BOTTOM: Denis, Dorothy and Colin McLoughlin dressed up for the town late 1950s.

rive one Sunday at their house as planned, Mac and Dorothy went over to his place to see if he was all right. After getting the police to break open the front door, they discovered Colin lying back in his armchair, blood on his chest and mouth. He had been dead for days.

They say bad things come in threes and they certainly did for Mac. It was not long after that traumatic discovery of Colin that yet more tragedy was to befall him. Dorothy began to suffer from a severe form of dementia; not only did her memory rapidly diminish but she became violent as well as physically strong. Mac would tell me how, during the night, she would begin to move heavy furniture about. Life became really challenging for him and, of course, his work suffered. He was no longer able to work nine hours a day, six days a week, drawing the *Commando* comics for D. C. Thomson, as so much of his time was taken up caring for his wife. This tragic burden was only lifted with Dorothy's sad death a few years later.

Ill fate still had not finished with Denis McLoughlin. During the nineties Mac had noticed the gradual decline in the neighbourhood where he lived. It had once been one of the finest areas in Bolton but now houses were rented and undesirable elements had moved in. Mac was sure that his new next-door neighbours were drug dealers. They certainly seemed to be full of criminal intent. After smashing his fence and throwing their garbage into his garden, they broke into his downstairs living room and trashed the place. Fortunately they didn't manage to get through into the upstairs part where Mac lived and worked as Mac had earlier reinforced the door in order to stop Dorothy from moving about at night and suffering an accident. He had at least eight break-ins as well as attempted break-ins. Despite notifying the police, nothing was done and he began to live on the edge of his nerves, at one time sleeping in a chair next to the front door with a revolver in hand (containing just one bullet), ready to defend his property.

Mac always believed in the sort of tough individuality so beloved of American movies wherein a man has a right to defend his property come what may. He thought it should be everyone's right to be allowed to arm

Continued on page 39

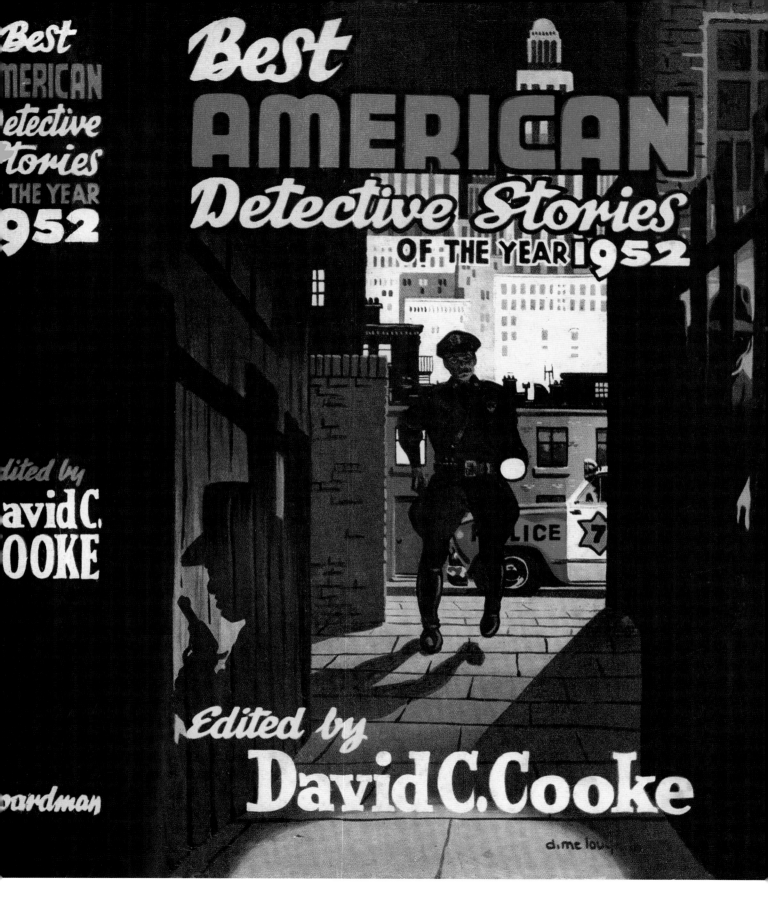

ABOVE: Cover to *Best American Detective Stories 1952*. Published April 1953.

ABOVE: *No Tears For Shirley Minton,* American Bloodhound Mystery 141, February 1957. The man with a gun and flashlight is a McLoughlin self portrait.

FACING PAGE: *Tweak the Devil's Nose,* Bloodhound Mystery 65, November 1953.

Tweak the DEVIL'S nose

Richard Deming

65

Boardman

A BLOODHOUND MYSTERY BY

Richard Deming

d. mc loughlin

ABOVE: *Run Killer Run,* **American Bloodhound Mystery 96, published February 1955.**

himself and believed that the Americans had got it right and that we should all possess guns. "Owning guns is a deterrent", he used to say. "A burglar's not going to come into your house if he thinks you've got a gun". This ultra right wing belief may be thought strange coming from someone who professed to be a Socialist through and through (the only politician I ever heard him praise was Tony Benn!) but that was Mac, full of contradictions.

There is no doubt that he loved all sorts of firearms. He often said that he had guns when he was young, as did his father. They were just kept in a drawer. As a mature artist, illustrating thrillers and Westerns, Mac had plenty of guns for reference but they were mostly replicas. His drawings and paintings of guns in the *Buffalo Bill Annuals* are among the most impressive in his oeuvre, delineated with such skill and obvious delight. At an early age I remember being fascinated by the trompe l'oeil paintings of guns in the second *Buffalo Bill Annual*, which appear to be pinned to the wall with tickets tied to them, telling you to which gunfighter they belonged! When I was able to put together something for Mac to illustrate for a *Look and Learn* annual, the title that immediately came into my mind was that of 'Guns and Gunfighters'! I suppose with hindsight it is not too surprising, though no less shocking, that when Mac decided to take his own life, he decided to use

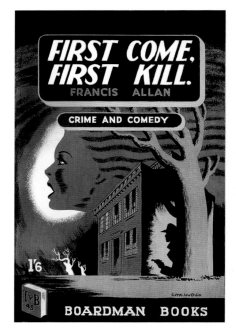

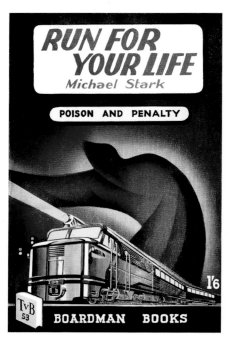

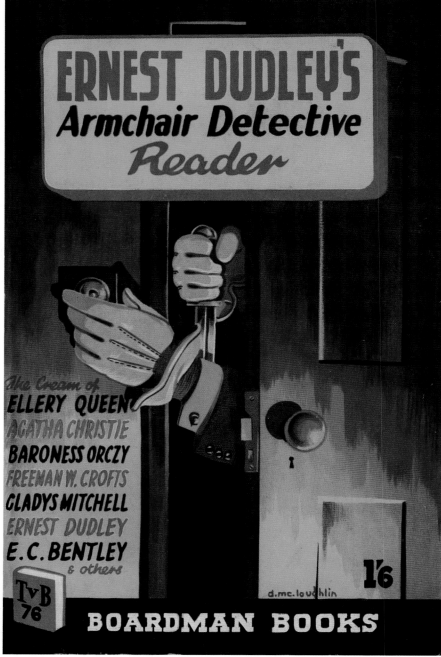

a pistol (the only non-replica gun he possessed) with its one bullet.

Denis McLoughlin died in 2002 at the age of 84. It appears that he might have been worried about the loss of feeling in his right arm, fearing that he wouldn't be able to draw again. This makes complete sense to me, as I know that drawing to Mac meant everything to him. He wouldn't have been able to envisage life without being able to carry on with his work.

Shortly after his death, I received an A4 envelope in the post from one of his relatives. Inside was a page of *Commando* artwork, together with a scrawled message he had written in capitals on a page of blotting paper. It simply said:

TOP LEFT: *First Come, First Kill,* **TVB paperback 45, 1949.**

TOP RIGHT: *Ernest Dudley's Armchair Detective Reader,* **TVB paperback 76, 1950.**

BOTTOM LEFT: *Run For Your Life,* **TVB paperback 53, 1948.**

Continued on page 45

ABOVE: *The Convertible Hearse*, **Bloodhound Mystery 218, July 1958.**

ABOVE: American Bloodhound 375 Lionel White *A Death At Sea* January 1962.

COMING DECEMBER 2012 FROM BOOK PALACE BOOKS

HEROS the SPARTAN

At last the book that comic strip aficionados have longed for finally sees print. Frank Bellamy's glorious artwork on *Heros the Spartan* has rightly achieved cult status, but the strip itself has never been reprinted in it's entirety until now. With an insightful introduction by Norman Boyd, interviews with Frank Bellamy and reproductions of Bellamy's working drawings as well as samples of original art, **Book Palace Books *Frank Bellamy's Heros the Spartan*** promises to be the ultimate statement on this lost treasure of British comic art.

Already published: ***Ron Embleton's Complete Adventures of Wulf the Briton*** has been described as "the book of the century", "stupendous, beautiful, amazing" and "the most impressive British comics reprint book ever". Drawing on interviews with friends and colleagues of the artist, reproductions from the original artwork and all the pages of the epic adventure meticulously restored and printed in the same huge dimensions as the original comic strip, ***Ron Embleton's Complete Adventures of Wulf the Briton*** is a must-have addition for the libraries of comic connoisseurs the world over.

43

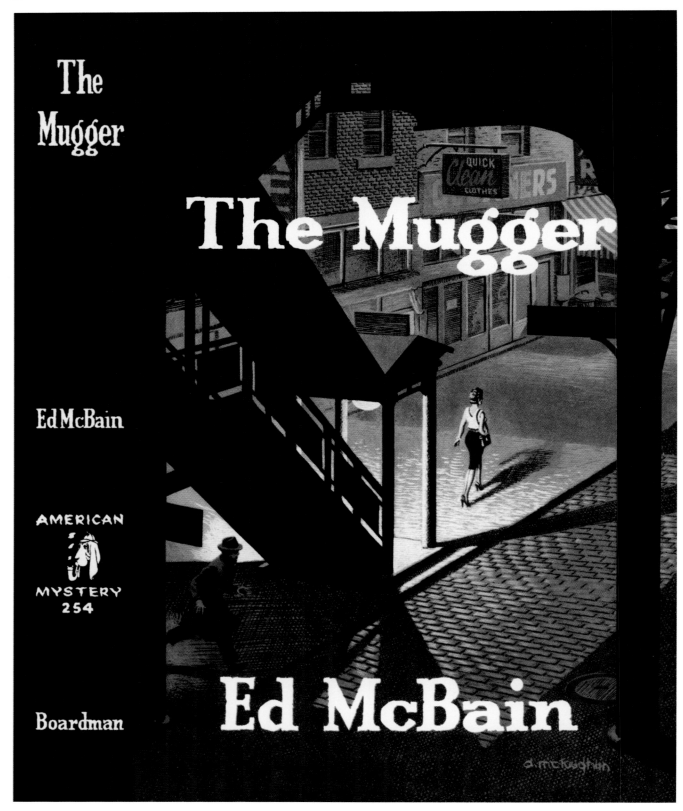

ABOVE: *The Mugger,* American Bloodhound Mystery 254, March 1959.

FACING PAGE: *Best American Detective Stories 1953,*
Boardman April 1954.

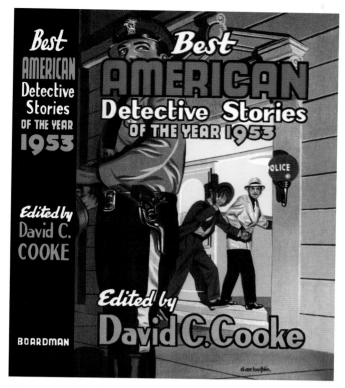

"Last page, don't send to Thomsons - David Ashford might like it". I often think he may have written this just before he picked up that revolver.

Later that same year, the BBC put out a documentary on *Buffalo Bill*, using many of McLoughlin's illustrations, and actually starting and ending the film with a shot of a boy propped up in bed, avidly reading with enjoyment and wonder the first *Buffalo Bill Annual*. I would have love Mac to have seen it. I know what his verdict would have been:- "Fabulous!"

-© David Ashford 2010

With many thanks to Mrs Janet Mason for her invaluable assistance in accessing much of the rare material that helped add to the scope and depth of this retrospective. She it was who literally rescued from certain oblivion much of Denis McLoughlin's proofs and reference photos as well as sketches, which had been consigned to his garden shed at the time of his death. Further thanks must be offered to Mark Terry and Gail Urbina of Facsimile Dust Jackets LLC for their assistance and expertise in adding extra sparkle to this feature with Mark's exquisite cover restorations and to Roger Peacey, Bill Pronzini, Michael Whale and Steve Taylor for providing scans of so many rare Bloodhound dustjackets.

ABOVE: Cover art for *Hot on the Trail, Commando 3046*. May 1997.

FACING PAGE TOP: The artist in his studio, reproduced by kind permission of The Courier, Dundee.

FACING PAGE: Portrait of the artist by friend and colleague Gordon Livingstone, who like Kennedy became one of the most distinctive artists working for DC Thomson's *Commando* comics.

Flights of Inspiration
An Interview With Ian Kennedy

Editor Peter Richardson conducted the following interview with Ian Kennedy in May of 2000 and it spans his years producing illustration and comic strip art for both Fleetway and D.C. Thomson as well as his many other commercial endeavours.

PR: To start at the beginning, you were telling me last week that you've just celebrated your first half century of commercial art.

IK: Well, certainly in the fifties, I think the half century will be up in August of this year (2000), if my arithmetic is correct. Starting August '49. No. That's right enough, it would have been last year I registered fifty wouldn't it? Arithmetic was never my strong point.

PR: I think it's often the way with artists, but before we get into your career can you give us a bit of background detail about yourself?

© Gordon Livingstone

© IPC Media

ABOVE: Two illustrations from *Quick on the Draw, Eagle Annual 5*, September 1955.

FACING PAGE: The final episode of *The Fastest Dustcart in the World*, published in *Express Weekly* January 4th 1958. Kennedy's visual dynamics are underpinned by his innate ability to put across a story.

IK: I was born in Dundee in 1932 and have never really strayed very far away from it. In fact the place I live in at the moment is on it's boundaries; a nice little place out in the country, which we've always wanted, nice and peaceful most of the time. Except when these noisy farmers are belting around in their tractors (laughs).

But I grew up in Dundee, had a normal sort of education, went through to what they call the Scottish higher stage, which is ... I don't know it's equivalent these days, probably getting on for the O-Level. I don't think it was ever quite as high a standard as the A-Level, but I did my Higher Art, never really with a view to going into art as a career. I was smitten early on, living through the war, watching all these lovely aeroplanes flying about, because we had quite a few airfields around the area ... and I wanted to fly as a career, and that was it! That was stalled very quickly, because I was also a very keen swimmer and apparently picked up an infection in the water, in the local swimming baths, which led to quite a lot of ear trouble, culminating in a mastoid operation. And that meant that flying was out, they wouldn't look at me. They didn't even want me for National Service. So that was that. It was a huge disappointment at a young age, but very fortunately the art was there and through a family connection I met a rather great character, David Ogilvie, who was an artist at D.C. Thomson's studio. He got me going very early on, before I was even away from school, into using pen and ink. This was a huge bonus, because it meant that when I did get into D.C. Thomson's quickly, about a month after leaving school, I was well acquainted with the pen and black ink. That was a huge boost at the time.

PR: Because people do get scared off by using ink, because they can't rub it out.

IK: That's right; it can be a very unsympathetic medium. The pen is an absolute...to use the word, sod. Still after all these years I find myself experimenting with various nibs, because I've found it depends very much on your state of mind. If you're a bit tense then the ink will just not flow off the nib. You can scratch and scratch and scratch and nothing will happen. At other times when you're quite relaxed, like everything else in life, it works very smoothly.

PR: You were using a pen well before you were using a brush?

IK: Yes...basically I was using pen and ink and of course, the brush and ink as well. I did no cover work at all until the late 1960s. So I was really twenty years into my career, before I was challenged by the colour cover.

PR: Right, because the colour cover is what you're now known for, but I remember, growing up one of the very first war comics I encountered was your *Birds of Prey* and I remember my brother and I looked at it and thought, "My God, this is amazing!"

IK: Was that *Air Ace*?

PR: Yes, really gorgeous, but I'm slightly racing ahead of where we should be, because before that you were working with D.C. Thomson and your first job there was ... very humble.

IK: Filling in the blacks on a Sunday Post crossword puzzle; yes that was my very first published work. Don't ask me which particular week it was or year. But it would obviously be somewhere in 1949/50. It was a case of being given a whole load of gridded papers and you stuck the numbers in the specified corners then blacked in the blacks according to the pattern. I think if I remember rightly, a lot of the ideas for the crossword, the actual plans etcetera were sent in by readers. Because I seem to remember working from quite rough sketches; somebody had lined it up and roughly pencilled in the black squares. That was my first published job!

PR: Well, from there they must presumably have eventually allowed you to draw figures and things that you're really brilliant at. Can you remember what your first comic was?

IK: Well, I really can't. I can only off the top of my head ... at that time picture stories weren't really in existence, apart from cartoons like *Oor Wullie* and *The Broons* and that sort of thing. You know the adventure picture story

ABOVE: *Hopalong Cassidy*, **June 8th 1957. Kennedy took over the feature when it was moved to the front page of Knockout.**

THE STORY SO FAR : Competing in the Two Thousand Miles across Europe, Dash Bennet and his assistant, Calculating Charlie, are pursued by crooks intent on retrieving their smuggled gold. One crook escapes with the Dustcart but crashes into a bridge . . .

© IPC Media

ABOVE Two pages from *The Kansas Kid*, one of several stories that Kennedy illustrated for *Cowboy Comics Library*.

had really just begun to come into being. At that time it was a case of the three column, four column story heading. In the likes of *Adventure, Rover, Hotspur, Wizard*. That was actually during the five years I was in the D.C. Thomson studio from '49 to '54.

PR: So you've actually done that apprenticeship of sitting at the desk.

IK: Oh very much so. In fact it's a strong belief I have that I was very lucky to serve in one of the last of a line of art studios which, to put it no higher, goes right the way back to the studios of Leonardo and Michaelangelo, where they took on young apprentices to fill in the corners of their great masterpieces. You sat and worked alongside very experienced men. I sit often these days, being a bit older myself, and think back to all these lovely guys; you know they were great fun. They were very experienced, many of them had served in the war of course. They did some marvellous stuff. When I wasn't doing stuff for publication I would go to this big chest of drawers at the end of the room in which all the original artwork lay, having been used and put away in these drawers, and I would pull one out and copy it line for line. And of course in passing they would often stop and have a look at it. Quite often the term they'd use was "Gosh! That's a beezer!" At other times when they saw where you were going wrong they would gently and sometimes not so gently point it out to you. A wonderful grounding. As far as I'm concerned it gave me the fundamentals for the rest of my life in art.

PR: I can think of many people who have never been to art college, who have learnt far more about the craft simply by working with people who have done it and are doing it.

IK: Hmmm ...I never did actually attend art college. I think if I remember rightly I did do one winter session right at the very start at the local art college in the evenings, but really my whole knowledge and experience has been built on that time in the studio with those professionals.

PR: So all these hard to master fundamentals such as figure drawing, perspective et al were learnt at D.C. Thomson?

IK: Oh very much so, with these guys.

PR: Really, so you never had life classes or drawing from the cast or people going into great discussions about anatomy.

IK: No, I was never part of that world at all.

PR: That's amazing because your figure work is done with such conviction.

IK: Don't you believe it! (laughs) Absolutely, even at this stage, I absolutely loathe figure work. It really does put me to the test!

PR: Well, ... er certainly a lot of younger artists do find figures very, very difficult but I think when you're doing comics, certainly your stuff does have that conviction. I'm just thinking about when you first started off in The Sun in the fifties you were doing *Billy the Kid*.

That's right. I seem to remember ... these things are all very vague I'm afraid. They come back to me from time to time. *Knockout* I think was the first with Amalgamated Press as it was in those days. Arthur Bouchier was the editor then. He was the first editor I worked for when I broke loose from Thomson's at the age of twenty-two and I did, I think it was, *Kit Carson*. Something like that, the Western strip story was very strong in those times.

PR: So you had to learn how to draw horses as well...

IK: Oh yes (laughs) ... you're reminding me of more torture.

PR: If it's any consolation, I'm remembering that story of Geoff Campion, whose style you had to emulate when you were drawing Billy the Kid. He told editor Leonard Matthews that he couldn't draw horses, to which Matthews replied. "Well, bloody well learn, then!"

IK: Laughs ... Oh God yes! Again going back to the studio business, one of the artists, a guy called George Ramsbottom, was very good at horses. He was probably ... they were all good draughtsmen, but he was the one I suppose I used as my icon. And he was good at westerns, horses and stagecoaches. So I tended to follow his lines on that. But horses ... OK, I don't buy (laughs), it wasn't like drawing Spitfires, put it like that.

ROCKED BY THE STORM OF HIGH EXPLOSIVE, SCARRED BY FLYING SHRAPNEL, THE LAST REMAINING BEAUFORT INCREDIBLY HELD ITS COURSE. EYES ON THE TORPEDO SIGHTS, SCRUFFY TURNER GRIMLY WAITED UNTIL THE RANGE CLOSED STILL FURTHER. THEN...

TORP GONE!

© IPC Media

ABOVE : *Birds of Prey, Air Ace 32,* **published December 1960.**

BELOW: The Battle of Britain, unpublished art painted for a private commission in 2002.

© IPC Media

PR: But talking of Spitfires, wasn't *Air Ace*, your first opportunity to tackle what you'd always wanted to do, these aeronautical ...

IK: Well, apart from the time I spent in the studio. Going back to that time, I was getting to be known as being keen on aeroplanes and any air stories that were going, again we're talking about story headings as opposed to picture stories, I tended to get them. But *Air Ace* as I recall, were the first of the picture stories, the air picture stories.

PR: They had a different editorial team to *War Picture Library* (Ted Bensberg), which was the first of the war oriented pocket libraries but *Air Ace* followed swiftly in it's wake and I think *Air Ace* was handled by a different editor, but there was nevertheless a great cross fertilisation of artists between the two titles.

IK: I'm desperately trying to recollect my visits south, to London, to IPC or AP, I can't remember when they changed names. I used to go to Farringdon Street, where the Amalgamated Press office was, but I think you're probably right, the two were separate entities.

PR: I think you became regarded as one of the primary exponents of these fantastic looking *Air Ace* stories with all these dashing young men leaping in and out of Spitfires.

IK: (Laughs) I think I was probably living my thwarted ambition through this situation. There was an awful lot of my yearning for that sort of thing went into my work. That sounds terribly pompous but I think that had a lot to do with it.

ABOVE: Superb example of Kennedy's ability to put the reader directly into the flying seat. A page from *Fighter Fighter, Air Ace 39*, February 1961, with a rare example of a Kennedy signature that managed to elude the Fleetway censor.

PR: Well, when we look at the stories that you worked on, I've got a list of your early ones and they got progressively more detailed. If you're looking at the pen work, the cross hatching and the disposition of tone and just the incredible feel of some of these pages, they still rank amongst the finest pages in action comics to this day. They've never been bettered.
Can you remember how long - it looks as if you must have given up living

much beyond the drawing board - how long did it take you to do one of these?

IK: I really quite honestly can't tell you ...er, I couldn't even guess now just how long it took me to do one of these. Er ... no off the top of my head Peter, I just cannot remember. I know that I always felt that OK I was going to be slower than some of the other guys who could dash it off and a lot of them could do it very convincingly. But I found that I couldn't do that so I just set to and got on with it.

PR: Well, it's like you were doing them as something very special and exceptional and something for yourself.

IK: Oh yes, it was something that I really did enjoy doing and I certainly did put all my heart and soul into it, I do know that.

PR: Did you do the lettering on some of them, because there are two or three of the earliest ones and the lettering is so distinctive and I've never seen it on any other artist's work.

IK: No, I never did any of the lettering at all. I think it was all done probably in-house. They may have had letterers working at home, but I certainly didn't do any. I remember once or twice, these may be the ones you're thinking of, there was a local guy who was looking for a bit of extra work and I did get him to do the lettering, so it could well be those are the ones that you're talking about.

PR: Some of the shots of Beauforts and Lancasters are so amazing, did you use kits at all?

IK: No. I have had the odd time when I was quite a keen aero-modeller, you know the Airfix kits and all that sort of thing, when I was younger. But I can't really say that I used them sitting there on the desk in front of me, as references. Maybe seeing them in the round, working on them, gave me a feel for the shapes, the perspectives and all the rest. But basically I've always worked from photographs. I've got a fairly extensive library here at home. Books by William Green and some of these marvellous Macdonald aeronautical publications full of good photographs. I don't think in many cases they've been bettered and they came out in, what, the sixties? These days the

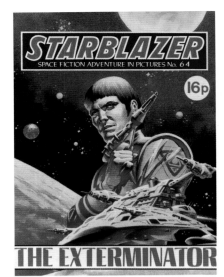

ABOVE: AND FACING PAGE
Samples of Kennedy's science-fiction
output. Five covers which appeared
from 1980 until 1982 from the fondly
remembered *Starblazer* series

stuff that's being published doesn't amount to much. It isn't as good as what was being published back then and yet there must be a great deal in the archives that could be brought out and printed.

PR: Going on from *Air Ace*, as it slowly declined your work began to appear in *War Picture Library*. Was that a bit of a wrench being forced to draw soldiers?

IK: (Laughs) If I remember rightly I didn't do too many of them did I?

PR: No, not an awful lot of them but I think from about the 400s on they began to appear in *War Picture Library*.

IK: Yes, ... Ted Bensberg was editor of *War Picture Library*, if I remember rightly. But again it all just disappears into my generally jumbled memory, where it was very busy and wonderful challenges all the time. What I term the Golden Times, the '60s and '70s when there was always something on the go. The phone never stopped ringing, which was marvellous ...wonderful.

ABOVE LEFT: A detail of the cover to *Space Watch* **one of the more unusual** *Commando* **scripts.** *Commando* **2774, July 1994.**

PR: Presumably you've always been busy since you first started with D.C. Thomson?

IK: Yes... again I consider it a wonderful stroke of luck that I've been able to live through these marvellous times and I was fortunate enough to be in contact with London and all the guys there, and it was always wonderful to go down and... You know, they were more than people one worked for, they became friends.

I still get the odd Christmas card from out of the blue and there are one or two others who still keep in contact. Most of them are out of the business now.

PR: But moving through the '60s and what happened in the '70s, which certainly affected your work, was the renaissance in science fiction, with *2000AD* and *Starlord*. And one of the favourite strips in *Starlord*, if not the favourite was your *Timequake*, which was beautiful.

OVERLEAF: Unnervingly prophetic double page spread from *Ro-Busters*. *Starlord* **5, published 10th June 1978.**

Continued on page 58

R.O.B.U.S.T.E.R.S

IK: Aah yes ... If I remember rightly I never did an awful lot for *2000AD* after the initial days, but *Starlord* was one I was involved in.

PR: Did you enjoy doing science fiction, because it's not exactly air war, but there are definite parallels there?

IK: Yes, I did. I found it a bit difficult at times, trying to get into the way-out, fantastic aircraft or spaceship design. That sort of thing I found a bit daunting, my mind really didn't run along these lines. And I had to work at it to get things to look fantastic, like these wonderful spaceships one saw in *Star Wars*. Suddenly I realised that these things didn't have to be streamlined, they could be all sorts of shapes. In fact I took to looking at things like lawn mowers and two stroke engines, just looking at the shapes then I started incorporating all these rather mundane shapes into a conglomerate and made a space ship out of it.

PR: Yes, it must have been liberating in a way to be freed of the need for specific reference.

IK: Yes, to coin a phrase, space is your oyster and, within reason, you can design almost anything providing it satisfies the requirements of the story.

PR: But by this time you were working in colour, which must have been a real liberation. It looks like you enjoyed it...

IK: It was a strange experience really. I think my first coloured cover was for a *Judy Library*, for Thomson's. A very good friend of mine was editor then, in fact I still meet him every Monday at a local hostelry and we have lunch. He has been retired now for ten, eleven years and he was the guy who gave me my first coloured cover. Very fortunately, I don't know how it came about, I came across acrylic colours at that time and I found them to be absolutely ideal for the purpose, in that you can use them like water-colours or oil and they have that wonderful vibrancy that is necessary for commercial art. Also coloured inks I used at that time too. In fact I think that particular cover I was talking about, the *Judy Library* one, was done with coloured inks. The acrylic colours came along shortly after that in time for my first *Commando* cover, which was sometime around 1969, '70 and they have been done solely in acrylics since then.

PR: Oh really...! Looking at them I thought that some may have been done in water-colour...

ABOVE TOP: *Pacific Peril, Judy Picture Story Library 62,* published 1969. The first of Kennedy's colour covers.

BOTTOM: Beautifully designed page from *Minnie's Mad Motor, Judy 718,* published 1973.

IK: This is a technique I've developed over the years. I started off with what they used to call a colour moulded technique, in other words you were using them like oils, building them up like an oil painting. That was OK and it was perfectly adequate for the purpose, but it was also rather time consuming. Over the years I've developed a technique using a dry brush drawing, initially coloured in over the top using a water-colour technique and then if necessary I can always thicken up the colour where I want to achieve the desired effect. In other words the tremendous versatility of the acrylic colours I find extremely useful.

PR: Were you using this acrylic technique on the comic strips as well...?

IK: Yes, it would be, yes definitely, although it might have been inks as well. With the like of *Starlord* it might well have been inks. I think with *Starlord* and the other strips I was doing at the time. It would have been inks on the smaller pictures. Really just doing a black and white drawing and washing in fairly flat tones of colour.

PR: But you also seem to use an airbrush from time to time as well.

IK: Never used an airbrush in my life. It's all done by the humble brush.

PR: You mentioned that you did your first *Commando* cover around 1968 or '69.

ABOVE: Ian Kennedy's debut *Commando* cover *Seek and Strike* published in January 1970. Painted shortly after the Judy cover, the artist dispensed with coloured inks and worked with acrylics.

ILLUSTRATION ART GALLERY

The world's largest selection of original illustration art

ABOVE: Ian Kennedy's *Tybalt* Which appeared in the Swedish comic *Fantomas* from 1990-2002.

© Egmont Serieforlaget AB

IK: Somewhere around about then, I have a note here somewhere, I had a quick look yesterday and I think it was number 453. Nine hundred and fifty covers yes... that's the ones I could count yesterday anyway. I've got all the proofs. I've kept them over the years.

PR: From my experience of *Commando*s you were appearing on a regular basis from the late '60s on, but saying that, am I right in thinking you've been much more evident over the last ten years or so?

IK: Yes,... I think that's probably the case. I don't know why that should be, whether or not the other guys who were involved have dropped out for some reason or other, I don't know. Of course the fact that I'm on tap here and can go into the office and discuss things with the editor probably is of some advantage to them.

PR: You still have this great affinity with air war stories, they're all lovely, but some of them such as *Night of Reckoning* with this magnificent view of a Lancaster bomber are so powerful. You just really seem to relish these air war stories...

IK: (Laughs) Oh very much so, my heart is still in the skies. I've done a bit of aeronautical painting in the past few years, thought about getting into the print side of things but, fortunately for me, I'm still kept busy on the commercial art side. I really haven't had the time or probably the inclination, because once you've finished work for the day or the week it's nice to get away from the drawing board. It might be different if I didn't have the commercial side, then perhaps the urge to do something on a grander scale would come back.

PR: You've never gone the whole hog and written the script as well?

IK: No I haven't, no I've never got round to doing that. I do work for an editor Ulf Granberg in Sweden and I did do a script for him once. It was accepted and that was quite satisfying... the story and the pictures.

PR: So you've got other outlets apart from *Commando* at the moment?

IK: Yes...in fact that is now the only other outlet. I did stuff for Semic Press

FACING PAGE: *They Fought By Night*, spectacular artwork for the cover of Commando 1585, published in 1982.

in Sweden, but they were bought over by another rather long sounding name Egmont Serieforlaget AB who still take a fair amount of my output as well.

PR: On the subject of output, how does your working day pan out?

IK: Well, generally speaking it's very much an office hours type of day. When I first went freelance, I was a young guy you know and full of the joys of life, loved going golfing. I thought this was a great idea, I'd do some work and then I'd be away out to the golf course. But I was soon pulled up very quickly by one of the directors of A.P. at that time, a chap called Monty Haydon. He said, "What's happening here, where's the work? You're contracted to do so much". I suddenly realised very quickly that the work came first and, if there was time left, then you could go out on the golf course. So...since then it's been very much an office type day, not quite so strict now, I'm easing off. But at the height of working, it would probably be a case of at the drawing board at eight in the morning and working on with two breaks for meals until the actual target for the day was met. If that took another couple of hours into the evening, then that was what was necessary.

PR: Yes, sure. So how long does it take on average to produce a cover?

IK: Well, it obviously depends very much on the content and the subject

OVERLEAF: *Night of Reckoning,* Ian Kennedy's powerful and atmospheric cover for *Commando 3009,* December 1996.

Continued on page 64

matter, but it can take on average about two days. Sometimes a bit less, but if you have a fair amount of action in it, including figures, then obviously that's going to take a bit longer.

PR: And also the uniforms and equipment, as one looks over your *Commando* covers, become more and more accurate. Is this because there is more material that you can draw upon these days for uniforms?

IK: Yes, I would say so. Again I have a fair amount of stuff here that I've built up over the years. One wall of my studio consists of bookshelves and is full of World War 2 references mainly. And, of course, if I need anything else they have a fairly good access in DC Thomson to material as well.

PR: Unlike Amalgamated Press/ Fleetway they have actually hung on to an awful lot of their artwork, which is nice to know that it hasn't been thrown away.

IK: Yes, that's the case. Although I have been told it's not the first time that an editor has been told to shred an awful lot of stuff, which is sad. It would have been nice to have got it back.

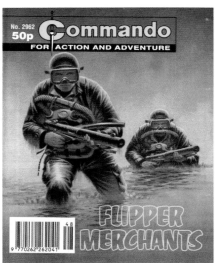

ABOVE TOP: *The Deadly Trade, Commando 2621, December 1992.*

BOTTOM: *Flipper Merchants, Commando 2962, June 1996.*

© IPC Media

PR: Well, presumably you never got the bulk of your Fleetway work back?

IK: Got very little of it back. In fact apart from one or two pages of *Dan Dare* which I did in the early '80's, I'm afraid the rest went walkies.

PR: Yes, not unusual. In fact a lot of the artwork just seems to have completely disappeared altogether. Including the bulk of all the pocket libraries.

IK: Yes, I can imagine. Whether or not the bulk of it was destroyed I just don't know.

PR: Looking to the future, are there any specific things you feel you'd like to do that you haven't done yet?

IK: Not really. I'm at the stage now where I'm semi-retired. I still do a three, three and a half day week, which is very nice as I'm still involved and keeping myself reasonably sharp hopefully. But I've no great ambitions at the moment. That's when I think to myself OK, when everything folds as it looks like it might do inevitably, I might just hang up the brush and say, "Well that's it." I say that and then realise there's got to be more to it than that. Probably, if I was going to be doing anything, it would be aeronautical painting, getting into the big stuff! It's very difficult having worked to commission all my life and would obviously demand a totally different mindset to sit down and just do things on spec. It's quite a problem Peter. I've thought about it often enough, but I just can't somehow or other, envisage the moment when that might happen.

PR: What influences did you have when you were growing up, Ian? In between wanting to be a Spitfire pilot you must have been thinking about wanting to be an artist as well?

IK: Not really, although my father often used to comment to his friends, "Give Ian the kitchen table after the evening meal and that's him quite happy till bedtime". You know, drawing and painting. Not so much painting, just drawing. And one of my earliest memories was that, if they wanted to keep me quiet, they would just give me a paper and pencil. But I can't honestly

ABOVE: Original art for *Lion* comic, published 9th October 1965.

say that, until the frustration of my ambition to fly, becoming a commercial artist, or any kind of artist working for a living, ever occurred to me. So, really and truly it was not until I was around fifteen, when it was obvious that the ear trouble was going to keep me out of flying, that it began to gel. Then meeting the artist (David Ogilvie) who was well established in Thomson's studio, I suppose that was when it all began to take shape.

PR: When you were working you must have had people that you rated quite highly...?

IK: Oh yes. There were always styles I admired. The way it was done. As I said earlier, the colleagues I worked

RIGHT: Cover to *Target - America!*, *Commando* 2936, February 1996.

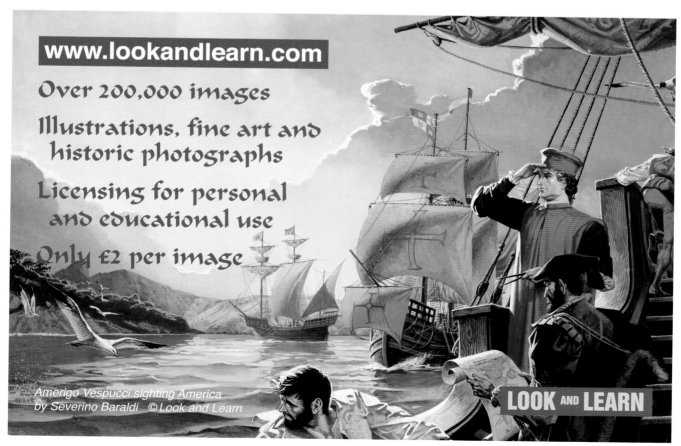

with in Thomson's. I can always remember being told something by the particular artist who introduced me to my career. He lived in another part of the town and as his mother lived in the next street to where I lived we used to meet there. On a wall in his mother's house, there was a little... I think it must have been a little etching. It was certainly black and white. It really was very simple, two or three lines and was actually, if I remember rightly, the bridge at Avignon. It really was so simple, I don't know what made me comment on it, because I was just a youth after all. But I did have to say, "Gosh, there's nothing there and yet you can see the picture." Dave did say to me at that time, "Yes the best artist always knows what to leave out."(laughs) I've been desperately trying to achieve that all my life. I still, I'm afraid, tend to overwork things, dot the I's and cross the T's. I think we all do (laughs). Someday I might just learn what to leave out!

BELOW: Cover for *The Long Night, Commando* 2136, published November 1987.

FACING PAGE: Cover artwork for *Joe The Jinx* published 1995

60s Chic

The Alluring Art of Angel Badia Camps
by David A. Roach

It is fitting that when the first foreign artist started drawing for the British comics industry in 1954 it was a Spaniard: Jesus Blasco. Of all the various nationalities who plied their trade over here it was the Spanish who were by far the most prolific. From the '50s to the '90s almost 400 Spaniards are known to have drawn strips for British comics, mostly through agencies such as Bardon, Norma, A.L.I., Creacciones and Selecciones Illustradas, better known by their initials S.I. These artists would often move from agency to agency, chasing better rates and more prestigious assignments but S.I had a core membership of highly talented young artists who electrified British comics in the '50s and '60s before doing the same in America with Warren comics and countless paperback covers. Interestingly, S.I's artists tended to follow a particular career trajectory where they would start off drawing small format Western or Science fiction strips (for syndication around Europe), before switching to higher paid British Romance or War features and then moving into commercial illustration and ultimately painting for Galleries. One artist, however, appeared to move between these various worlds at will, switching from painting to comics and back again, just as he effortlessly moved between agencies and genres. His name is Angel Badia Camps.

Camps was born in 1929, which makes him one of the older members of what some have called the golden generation of Spanish comic artists, a generation that grew up in the aftermath of a Civil War which left their country both isolated and considerably poorer than the rest of Europe. Interestingly, many of these artists were born and worked in Barcelona, which must have had the highest density of comic book artists anywhere in the world. The biggest publisher in the '50s was Bruguera and like, so many other artists, much of Camps' formative work appeared in their titles, such as Pulgarcito and Aventuras De Capa Negra. Amongst his earliest paintings would appear to have been a series of covers for the girls' comic *Sissi* which also featured early work by Antonio Bernal, Manuel Brea and Antonio Bosch Penalva. However, the Spanish industry paid relatively poorly so, when the opportunity arose to work for the more lucrative British market ,many artists, Camps included, jumped at the chance. Differences in

ABOVE: *True Life* 510, 1966 and issue 556, 1967

the exchange rate between Sterling and the Peseta meant that artists could earn as much as three times their usual Spanish page rate and though many came to loath the unending succession of romance strips they had to draw most made a very good living out of them nonetheless.

When the Spanish artists hit Britain they were a revelation. Though many were very young and barely out of their teens, they had an astonishingly assured grasp of anatomy and draughtsmanship coupled with a sophisticated rendering which made most of the British artists look decidedly old fashioned by comparison. The Spanish were quickly typecast as either Romance (S.I's Barcelona based studio) or War (Bardons' Valencia studio centred around Luis Bermejo) artists, though some such as Jose Ortiz were versatile enough to move freely across all manner of genres. In the romance genre by far the most influential artist was Jorge Longaron (later to find fame in the U.S. drawing the *Friday Foster* newspaper strip) whose elegant, stylish drawing and stunning girls looked thrillingly modern. Britain's often inward looking, parochial industry of the '50s was largely made up of newly demobbed youthful enthusiasts, rapidly establishing an artistic identity along with a less adventurous conglomeration of journeymen and artisans from the contracting worlds of pre-war illustration and story papers. The latter were typically shunted towards the nascent romance lines, with largely uninspiring results. Longaron's earliest strips started appearing in 1957, primarily in the pages of *Valentine* (along with fellow pioneers Carlos Prunes and Jose Maria Miralles), and he brought with him the energy of American comic books and the refinement of Alex Raymond's *Rip Kirby*. Stan Drake's groundbreaking *Juliet Jones* newspaper strip was also an early influence and by the 60s S.I's studio was awash with illustrations by American artists such as Coby Whitmore, Al Parker and Joe Bowler, which proved to be enormously influential. Longaron distilled these various approaches into a style that largely threw away traditional cross-hatched pen work or feathered brush strokes. Instead he was all about vibrant, energetic lines, pared–down inking, abstract shapes, negative space and realistic figure drawing. He created a style that would dominate Romance comics for over a decade, until the lighter, more cartoon-like drawing style of Purita Campos came to prominence. Of the many artists to follow Longarons lead none came as close to his standard as Camps

Pinning down specific dates in the career of Angel Badia Camps is a tricky affair as little biographical information has appeared in print, but it would appear that sometime in 1961 he moved over to S.I and later that year his first comic strips appeared in *Valentine*. For the next 6 years his strip work was featured in *Valentine*, *Serenade*, *Roxy* and in two 64 page issues of *True Life* stories (issues 387 and 396, his two longest strips). At first glance his drawing style was almost indistinguishable from Longaron's as he mixed a thrillingly loose and expressive line with an inventive and sophisticated sense of composition. His girls were the very epitome of "the Spanish look" – heavy lidded, thickly mascara'd eyes, big hair, big lips and lithe, languid bodies. It is worth noting that Camps assiduously tried to make his strips look as British as possible, even travelling to the UK where he took over 300 reference photos. His work on *Serenade* was particularly interesting because its covers featured a limited amount of colour which allowed him to be wonderfully bold and inventive. Camps' work here is some of the very best in the genre. His line work was if anything even more expressive than Longaron's, but perhaps the best way to tell the two apart is in their depiction of women. Longaron's female leads were gamin, playful, girl next door types, whereas Camps' women exuded

ABOVE: *Serenade* 4, 13th October 1964.

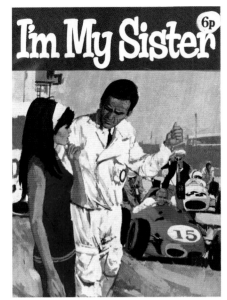

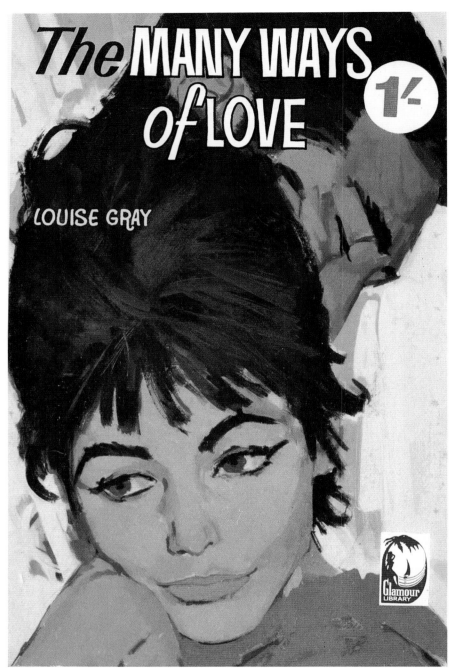

TOP LEFT: *Romantic Adventure Library* 279 (undated, but probably late 60's)

TOP RIGHT: *Oracle Library* 375 1965

BOTTOM LEFT: *Glamour Library* 357 1964

FACING PAGE: Main image- *Romantic Adventure Library* 655, reprinting a cover originally painted for *Pop Pic Library*, mid 1960s. Smaller images, *Star Love Stories* 193 1967, 596 1975, 664 1977

an exotic froideur, as they looked down their noses at their pitiful, male prey. It would seem that his final work for *Valentine* in 1967 was also his final work in comics as painting, which had taken up much of time during that period, would become his sole focus for the rest of his life

Most of S.I's artists worked in the company's office in the centre of Barcelona on Las Ramblas, in two large, top floor rooms. However, Camps preferred to work at home, which perhaps allowed him greater freedom to explore other ventures (and other agencies). While

his strips first saw print in 1961 his earliest covers had appeared the previous year in *The Sexton Blake Library*. Between 1960 and 1967, through 100s of covers for *True Life, Star Love, Love Story, Oracle, Pop Pic Library, Charm, Young Lovers* and many, many others he proved himself one of the most talented artists of his generation. Looking at his painted work it is clear that here was a great illustrator creating magazine quality artwork for comic books. There were strong similarities with the likes of Al Parker, Mitchell Hooks and particularly with Joe Bowler. The drawing and painting was thrillingly accomplished, but it was married to an invention and sense of adventure that saw him playing around with figures as shapes in a very exciting way. Looking at a cover such as *Night Must End* or *Guy With Go* there is a real sense that here is someone at the very top of his game, pushing the focus of the painting to its edges, using negative space, extreme close-ups, asymmetrical compositions, flat colours, textures. You name it, it's here. Of the many Spaniards painting covers for the romance market Camps was unquestionably the best.

Stylistically, in this period Camps was very much working in what might be called the "Cooper Studio Style", that is to say the technique typically used by the artists of the Charles E. Cooper Studio in New York City in the 1950s and 60s. The Cooper artists were the most inventive in America with figures such as Joe De Mers, Coby Whitmore,

Lynn Buckham, Joe Bowler and Robert Jones dominating the lucrative and stylish Women's magazine market with their romantic "boy/girl" compositions. Eschewing the more traditional, richly rendered oil painting tradition of a Rockwell or Cornwell, the Cooper Studio artists preferred the stark immediacy of gouache and their fiction illustrations became increasingly more focused on decoration, design and innovation than a strictly representational approach. Camps was absolutely part of this new direction and his romance covers were the very epitome of 1960's nouvelle chic.

Like his American counterparts Camps worked in gouache, usually laying down an often white, monotone background and building up the main figures with broad, confident brush strokes. There was no attempt at subtle gradations of tone; the paint was put on in angular blocks with more precise details reserved for faces and hands. On seeing a Camps original it is striking quite how rough and gestural the painting is; clearly he was perfectly aware of how the image would soften and blend in reproduction. For clothing he adopted a stylised approach with a single base colour accented with design elements such as stripes or patterns with a few deft indications of creases, folds and shadows suggesting weight and solidity. In an almost oriental approach these illustrations were essentially an assembly of flat shapes with just enough rendering to give them the illusion of depth. This more impressionistic approach worked so well for Camps because of

TOP: *Love Story 487, 1964.*

BOTTOM: *Can't Fall In Love,* *True Life 442, 1964*

the quality of his drawing, of his understanding of lighting and his inventive designs. Essentially his emphasis was on shapes, the juxta-positions of patterns and breathtakingly beautiful faces. Background elements were invariably subservient to the focus on the romantic couple and were pared down to the minimum. For city scenes Camps favoured artfully angled lamp posts or railings, interiors were often just chairs, staircases, artfully arranged fabrics or lamps: whatever it took to provide a context while never disrupting the rhythm or de-sign of the picture. With their Beehive hairdos and mini skirts these covers are clearly of their time and yet they still resonate today and remain the creative pinnacle of Camps' commercial career.

Interestingly, while these covers seemingly represent swinging London in all its grandeur and frivolity, it might well be the case that none of them were specifically created for the British market at all. While his strips were directly commissioned through S.I his cov-ers appear to have been painted for rival agencies A.L.I and Bardon. Bardon had strong links with the Scandinavian market and typically would sell first printing rights for artwork to Swedish or Norwegian publishers, then reselling the images all over Europe. Consequently many of Camps' covers started life as women's magazine illustrations

TOP: Women's magazine illustration.

BOTTOM: *Promise In A Kiss, Love Story 479, 1964.*

TOP: Women's magazine illustration.

BOTTOM: Spanish Enid Blyton book cover

and were then sold on to *Love Story*, *Star Love* or *True Life* a few years later. Even within Britain itself a lot of recycling went on with publishers endlessly reprinting and repackaging their material. For instance the cover of *Pop-Pic Library* No. 33 *All Or Nothing* shows the titles' rather overpowering recurring motif of a large guitar filling the left side. Years later another *Pop Pic* cover was utilised for *Romantic Adventure Library* with less than wonderful results – the painting is terrific but now features two gorgeous '60s chicks apparently staring at a vast expanse of brown where once the guitar would have been. Even one of his very earliest *Sexton Blake* covers is known to have also appeared on a Spanish detective paperback. This recycling also spun out further as other crime illustrations were re-sold through the Ortega agency to the German publishing house Pabel for its *Komissar X* series. In amongst the Romance and Crime it would appear that Camps still retained links with Bruguera and somehow found the time to beautifully illustrate a series of altogether more genteel fares such as *Heidi* and *Treasure Island*.

Despite the popular perception that comics were the poor relations of illustration, Camps seems to have been quite happy to work on both strips and illustrations throughout the decade. Beginning in the

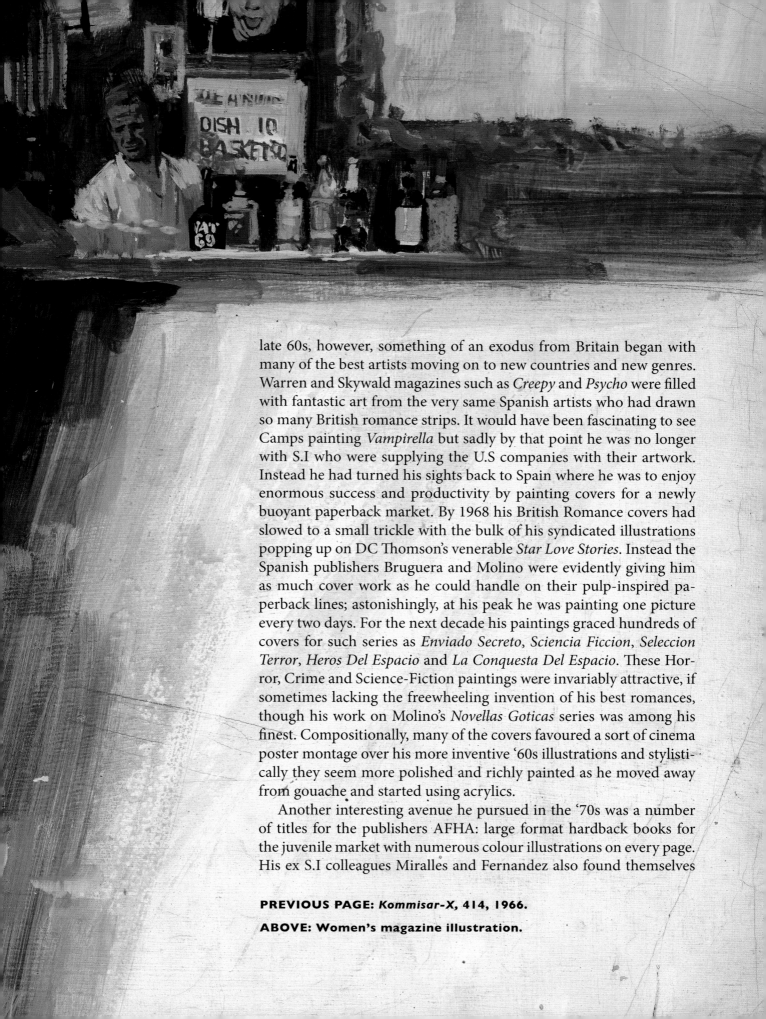

late 60s, however, something of an exodus from Britain began with many of the best artists moving on to new countries and new genres. Warren and Skywald magazines such as *Creepy* and *Psycho* were filled with fantastic art from the very same Spanish artists who had drawn so many British romance strips. It would have been fascinating to see Camps painting *Vampirella* but sadly by that point he was no longer with S.I who were supplying the U.S companies with their artwork. Instead he had turned his sights back to Spain where he was to enjoy enormous success and productivity by painting covers for a newly buoyant paperback market. By 1968 his British Romance covers had slowed to a small trickle with the bulk of his syndicated illustrations popping up on DC Thomson's venerable *Star Love Stories*. Instead the Spanish publishers Bruguera and Molino were evidently giving him as much cover work as he could handle on their pulp-inspired paperback lines; astonishingly, at his peak he was painting one picture every two days. For the next decade his paintings graced hundreds of covers for such series as *Enviado Secreto*, *Sciencia Ficcion*, *Seleccion Terror*, *Heros Del Espacio* and *La Conquesta Del Espacio*. These Horror, Crime and Science-Fiction paintings were invariably attractive, if sometimes lacking the freewheeling invention of his best romances, though his work on Molino's *Novellas Goticas* series was among his finest. Compositionally, many of the covers favoured a sort of cinema poster montage over his more inventive '60s illustrations and stylistically they seem more polished and richly painted as he moved away from gouache and started using acrylics.

Another interesting avenue he pursued in the '70s was a number of titles for the publishers AFHA: large format hardback books for the juvenile market with numerous colour illustrations on every page. His ex S.I colleagues Miralles and Fernandez also found themselves

PREVIOUS PAGE: *Kommisar-X*, 414, 1966.

ABOVE: Women's magazine illustration.

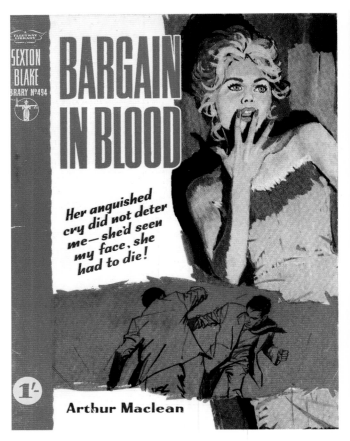

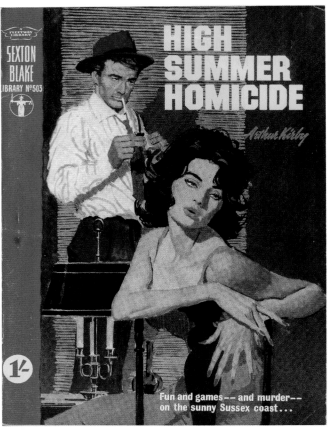

CARIBBEAN CRISIS

He went on a lone mission to a sun-drenched island of violence and bloodshed, corruption and political intrigue...

Desmond Reid

ABOVE: *Sexton Blake* 494, 501 and 503, published 1962.

at AFHA and Camps' work on such titles at the *Conquest of Space* and *The Bible* was every bit as attractive as theirs. The artist had earlier dabbled in the children's book market with a series of attractive Enid Blyton covers for Molino but in the Late '70s and early '80s much of his time was devoted to the genre. For the Toray publishing house he painted numerous covers for girls' series such as *Puck*, *Fantomette* and the books of Maria Luisa Fischer. Over at Molino the fare was largely aimed at boys, including such series as *Encyclopedia Brown*, *Tom Swift*, *Michel Investigore*, *Alfred Hitchcock's Three Investigators* (for which he painted nearly 30 covers) and *Guillermo* or, as we know him, *Just William*. However, Camps was nothing if not prolific and this period also saw him create covers for such authors as Agatha Christie, Malcolm Saville, Charles Dickens and Earl Stanley Gardner as well as for numerous Westerns. Clearly the Camps completist needs both great persistence and deep pockets.

As the market for painted book covers contracted in the '80s and '90s (and, perhaps more to the point, the artist grew tired of the commercial grind), Camps moved into fine art and academia, setting up his own art school with fellow comic book/paperback artist, Rafael Cortiella, which the pair ran for over ten years. In recent years he has concentrated on gallery paintings, which fall into several categorie: still-lifes, buildings or cityscapes, children, portraits or nudes. All of which are equally stunning. As an aside, it is fascinating to see so

many Spanish artists taking exactly the same career moves. The likes of Jordi Longaron and Warren favourites Felix Mas, Fernando Fernandez, Luis Garcia Mozos and Leopoldo Sanchez have all emerged as major talents in the Gallery arena. In an interview with the Elrincon blog site Camps has recently revealed quite how his move into fine art came about. It seems that one day, while painting on holiday a gallery owner chanced upon the artist and asked if he had any more paintings. Despite the artist's protestations that he was only a "Sunday painter" Camps relented and took his admirer back to his apartment to see the rest of his pictures. The gallery owner bought the lot and a new career was born. While there is a certain continuity between his comic and paperback works, Camps' gallery paintings clearly belong to a different tradition of contemporary realism.

In an art world where the avant-garde has become the mainstream, it is fascinating to see that an alternative "movement" of realist, photo-realist or neo-impressionists is operating in parallel, seemingly below the radar of most critics. These are artists educated in America's more rigorously traditional art colleges or ateliers, Chinese art schools or European refugees from the commercial sphere. Typically they would trace their artistic lineage from painters such as John Singer Sargent (definitely a touchstone figure for many contemporary realists) and

© IPC Media

TOP: Women's magazine illustration.

BOTTOM: *Heart String Serenade, Love Story 473, 1964.*

ABOVE TOP: Women's magazine illustration.

ABOVE: *Only One Love, True Life* **563, 1967.**

Anders Zorn, through twentieth century figures such as Andrew Wyeth, Nicolai Fechin and Euan Uglow to modern artists, including Jenny Saville, Antonio Lopez, Gerhard Richter and, particularly, Lucien Freud. The success and critical acclaim of Freud suggests that there might well be a reopening of interest in figurative work, which could conceivable see Camps emerge as a leading figure in the art world. His figure paintings typically feature a lone figure, usually a nude or partially clothed woman, in a sparsely furnished room. He shares with Freud an acute sense of observation coupled with a chilly, bleached out tonality. Many of these works exude a kind of pensive melancholia, light years removed from the exuberance of his romance period. His urban landscapes share the acute vision of Antonio Lopez or Freud and are another example of his transition from the commercial to the fine art world. In these new pieces the artist is clearly reaching towards pictures of great depth and meaning, touching on profound insight.

Camps may have left behind his pulp roots but his vision and creativity are still as inspired as ever.

David A. Roach 2012

iQ COMING ATTRACTIONS:

In the next issue of **illustrators**: *My Affair With Carol Day*. Roger Clark and Peter Richardson examine the life and work of the UK's foremost postwar glamour illustrator, David Wright. Drawing on interviews with colleagues and family, **illustrators** presents and contextualises Wright's seductive and atmospheric artwork and the world of Fitzrovian mystique that it so perfectly encapsulates.

Future issues of **illustrators** will focus on the work of *Fortunino Matania, Reginald Heade, Mick Brownfield, Brian Sanders, John Watkiss, Pauline Baynes, Luis Garcia Mozos, John Millar Watt, Leslie Ashwell Wood, Ron Embleton, Raymond Sheppard, Anne and Janet Grahame Johnston, Jordi Penalva, Roger Coleman, C.L. Doughty, Patrick Nicholle, Eric Parker , Graham Coton* and *Walter Wyles.*

To avoid missing this or any other issue of **illustrators** subscribe today:
Four Issue Subscriptions:
£55 post free UK
£77 airmail Europe
£89 airmail USA/rest of world

FRANK BELLAMY

An ongoing collection of books devoted to one of the greatest graphic story tellers the world has ever seen. Available from **Book Palace Books**.

The Gallery

Sensuous Sensibility

The Fin de Siècle Erotica of Cheri Herouard

by David A. Roach

FACING PAGE: Cover to *La Vie Parisienne* 30th October 1920.

The French artist better known as Cheri Herouard was born in 1881 with the appropriately florid and romantic name of Darling Louis Marie Aime Haume. After his father's premature death, the young Darling adopted his stepfather's surname of Herouard. Fittingly his long artistic career was itself characterized by changing personalities and hidden identities. Herouard was possessed of a wonderfully clean, painstakingly detailed style whose precision and seeming lack of guile concealed a profoundly erotic sensibility. His earliest illustrations were created for *Le Journal De La Juenesse* and *Semaine De Suzette* where his clarity of line was perhaps reminiscent of another great children's book illustrator, Boutet De Monvel. However, in 1907 he started a 45 year association with the altogether more scurrilous *La Vie Parisienne,* which gave him free reign to explore his adoration for the female form. Here his gloriously-drawn nymphs could be found either extravagantly bedecked in meticulously rendered costumery or innocently cavorting in the nude, frequently leered at by be-warted peasants, or frolicking with mythical creatures.

La Vie Parisienne was a glossy, tabloid sized weekly which mixed humorous text with drawings and full page illustrations, much as the British *Punch* did. However, being French, the magazines over-riding preoccupation was with pretty girls and sex. *La Vie* featured many talented artists such as George Leonnec, Raphael Kirchner and George Barbier, but Herouard was by far its greatest talent. His many covers and centrespreads were a symphony of delicate watercolours, marbled flesh, obsessive decoration and winsome beauty, conjured up in his distinctive, seemingly contradictory, style of innocent sexuality. Herouard worked at *La Vie* until he was 71 but while it was the most visible venue for his artwork he was immensely versatile and prolific elsewhere as well.

His light hearted but realistically rendered illustrations made him a natural for posters, postcards and menus and he was often found advertising wines or

LA JALOUSIE

LA VIE PARISIENNE

HEROUARD

TOUT À LA CHINE OU LE DERNIER DADA

58e Année. N° 10-15   Le Numéro : UN franc   6 Mars-10 Avril 1920

LA VIE PARISIENNE

Au Théatre
des Quatre Saisons

Le Printemps
entre en scène

HEROUARD

Rédaction, Administration et Publicité : 29, rue Tronchet, Paris.

55e Année. N° 15   Le Numéro : 60 centimes   Samedi 14 Avril 1917

LA VIE PARISIENNE

Bagdad

Hérouard

Rédaction, Administration et Publicité : 59, rue Tronchet, Paris.

ABOVE: Cover to *La Vie Parisienne* 23rd October 1920.

restaurants. In addition to *La Vie* his art could also be found in such journals as *Le Sourire* and *Fantasio* but much of his time was devoted to illustrating books. While he often took on children's books such as *L'Heure De Grace* (in 1929) or *Pataud* (1945), much of his book work was suffused with an erotic sensibility. These included *Les Liasons Dangereuses*, *Mademoiselle De La Valiere* and *Le Jardin Enchante*. Perhaps his most impressive book project was *Les Ballades De Maitre* issued in a signed edition of 550 copies and filled with line illustrations of the highest quality, mixing beautiful girls with another of his great loves, historical illustration. The man of many names also adopted the pseudonym Herric for other, more specialised literary projects, such as *L'Infernale Fouettesse* and *Cinglants Chatiments*. These were books devoted to Bondage and domination and Herouard/Herric's drawings were at once charming and shocking; charming in their beautiful delineation and shocking for their scenes of whippings and spankings. Smut has never looked so beautiful. Herouard died in 1961 and is today an undeservedly obscure figure. However copies of *La Vie Parisienne* with his artwork on their covers are quickly snapped up when offered for sale, so pockets of admirers are still around.

David A Roach. Feb 2012

ABOVE: Detail from centrespread of *La Vie Parisienne* 5th May 1917.

ABOVE TOP: The many faces of Eve from *La Vie Parisienne* 9th December 1922.

The Studio

Daleks, Dancers and Decorations

Mick Brownfield describes how he he set about creating one of his most iconic Radio Times Christmas covers

When I received a call from Radio Times Art Director Shem Law, in October 2009, it was quite a surprise. He asked me if I would like to submit some ideas for that year's Christmas cover (as if I wouldn't). I hadn't done a cover for over 10 years. The '90's had been a golden decade for me and the BBC. I had done 5 Christmas covers and countless other jobs, big and small, for them, and was on first-name terms with everyone.

This flow of work was reduced to a trickle by 2009, as the use of illustration seemed to be frowned upon. All that was left were postage stamp-sized drawings for the radio pages, and the annual festive cover.

Twenty years ago the creative process involved lunch/tea with the Editor and head design staff. After a couple of hours we decided on an idea and I would go off happily to start work.

Computers have now made the need for face-to-face meetings largely redundant, so I agreed to cook-up 2 or 3 'concepts', while being warned that 3 other illustrators would be doing the same thing.

A couple of ideas were dismissed, and then I started thinking about tin

toys..... Christmassy and fun to draw. I liked the idea of Santa winding up a toy version of himself. This is when the real 'wind up' began. The Editor liked my sketch but thought the toy depicted should reflect the big seasonal programmes. Hence, *Dr Who (Dalek)* and *Strictly* (dancing couple). Two different covers meant 2 overlays as I couldn't face painting the same Santa twice. They also asked for separate tree decorations, which were never used.

Before I began, I dove into my well-thumbed Haddon Sundblom book, to get me in the mood. For me his version of Santa is supreme. It took me about 7 days to complete the artwork. I scanned it and sent it off. All this extra work meant a double fee, so I was paid handsomely for doing what I think of as the premier job of the year for any illustrator.

The end result was much liked by all at the BBC, and remains my favourite Christmas cover - so far!.

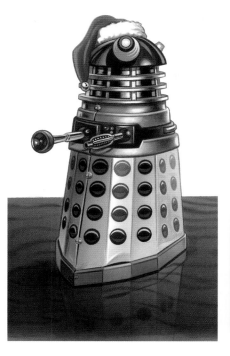

The Bookshelf

Robert Fawcett: The Illustrator's Illustrator
by David Apatoff. Hard-bound 182 pages. Auad Publishing £27.99

This is a book which Fawcett connoisseurs have long been awaiting. If ever an illustrator was overdue for a major reassessment of his life and work it has to be Fawcett. Apatoff's book doesn't disappoint, besides a superb selection of Fawcett's illustrations and working drawings, his text reveals a man who was a dedicated professional, whose integrity was such that despite the pressures of commerce, he exercised his own criteria in determining how his art was to be applied, even if it meant that he had to turn away otherwise lucrative work.

Frank Hampson: Tomorrow Revisited
by Alastair Crompton. Hard-bound, 214 pages. PS Art Books £29.99

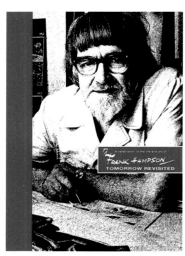

Another artist whose integrity overruled the commercial imperative is Frank Hampson. He is the man responsible for revitalising the largely moribund post war UK comics industry through the creation of the superbly drawn and scripted Dan Dare. As Crompton's compelling text reveals there was, however, a darker side to the story behind Dan Dare, which manifested itself in the obsessive and demanding production methods that Hampson required to produce the requisite volume of work for this ground-breaking strip. Crompton's gripping text is further enriched by superb reproductions of some of the finest examples of the Hampson studio's original artwork for the strip that beget a new generation of space-bedazzled readers. There is also a slip-cased limited edition with an original watercolour drawing by Don Harley - if you can get your hands on one. £295

Masters of American Illustration: 41 Illustrators and How They Worked.
by Fred Taraba. Hard-bound 432 pages. The Illustrated Press £39.99

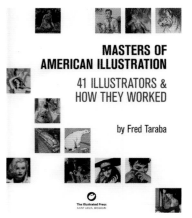

The Illustrated Press continues with its mission to focus attention on some of the greatest illustration ever to have been produced. Fred Taraba's *Masters of American Illustration: 41 Illustrators and How They Worked* is a true labour of love and one of the most important books on illustration to have ever been produced. The product of years of research, the book takes a look at the working methods and lives of illustrators whose work reflected the seismic changes that were shaping the world they inhabited. Taraba spotlights many influential illustrators who for a variety of reasons have fallen beneath the radar of previous publications. What greatly adds to the appeal of this book, and makes it a necessity for every art college library, are the captions which accompany the exquisitely reproduced artworks, many of which are scanned from original art. Taraba's captions offer an incisive analysis of how each illustration is staged as well as the materials employed, which adds a whole new dimension to the appreciation of the artworks he is presenting. This book is an absolute must for any student and/or enthusiast of illustration.

Wally Wood's EC Stories Artist Edition

Written by Feldstein and Kurtzman. Illustrated by Wallace Wood. Hard Cover 152 Pages IDW £125

Stupendous and gigantic collection of the late, great Wally Wood's EC stories. Scanned from the original art in full colour so that editorial annotations, blue pencil, yellowing art board are all clearly visible and printed at the same size as the original boards, this book is probably the closest you will ever get to owning some of the finest Wood art ever. The ultimate statement on one of the most exciting graphic story artists ever. Definitely one of the books of the decade if not the century.

Harvey Dunn: Illustrator and Painter of the Pioneer West

Hard-bound, 304 pages. Flesk Publications £45

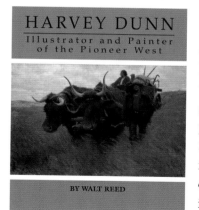

Acclaimed art historian Walt Reed presnts a masterful analysis of Harvey Dunn's work with his vivid and engaging text. Now it is possible to view nearly 300 of Dunn's artworks in colour. The amount of research involved in tracking down so many of Dunn's originals shows just how determined the team at Flesk publishing were in ensuring that this book would provide an enduring testimony to Dunn's art. They have proven themselves more than equal to the task and in doing so have produced a truly exceptional book on a monumental artist.

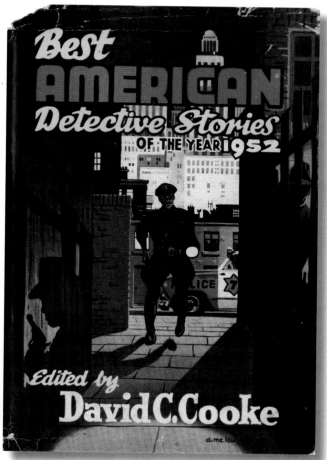

The Source

Online illustration Information

illustrationartgallery.blogspot.com
bookpalacebooks.blogspot.com
cloud-109.blogspot.com
bearalley.blogspot.com
lookandlearn.com/blog
britishcomicart.blogspot.com
frankbellamy.blogspot.com
goldenagecomicbookstories.blogspot.com
downthetubes.net
illustrateurs.blogspot.com
mirabilis-yearofwonders.blogspot.com
pocketwarcomics.blogspot.com
todaysinspiration.blogspot.com
lambiek.net
linesandcolors.com
illustrationart.blogspot.com
magazineart.org
mcginnispaintings.com
carol-day.com
tikit.net
muddycolors.blogspot.com
nocloo.com
howardpyle.blogspot.com

Image Libraries

lookandlearn.com
maryevans.com
bridgeman.co.uk

Galleries/ Museums

delart.org
nrm.org
cartoonart.org
www.coningsbygallery.com
www.gallerynucleus.com
somagallery.co.uk
brandywinemuseum.org

Where To Buy illustration Art

illustrationartgallery.com
tarabaillustrationart.com
graphiccollectibles.com
ramaguirecoverart.com
illustrationcupboard.com
booksillustrated.com
wow-art.com
ha.com
stuartngbooks.com
illustrationhouse.com
chrisbeetles.com

Publishers of illustration Books

bookpalacebooks.com
fleskpublications.com
auadpublishing.com
bpib.com
illustration-magazine.com
illustration-mag.com
bearalleybooks.blogspot.com/
pspublishing.co.uk/ps-art-books

Events

Cartoon Art Museum
Darth Vader and Son
28 April – 5 August 2012
Presentation and booksigning with Jeffrey Brown:
Thursday, 17 May 2012, 7:00-9:00pm
What, Me Worry? 60 Years of MAD
21 April – 16 September 2012
www.cartoonart.org

The Cartoon Museum
H M Bateman: The Man Who Went Mad On Paper
11 April 2012 – 22 July 2012
www.cartoonmuseum.org

Brandywine River Museum
A Painter's View: The Andrew Wyeth Studio
Until October 2012
www.brandywinemuseum.org

Norman Rockwell Museum
Howard Pyle: American Master Rediscovered
9 June through 28 October 2012
Norman Rockwell Sports!
6 July through 28 October, 2012
www.nrm.org

Delaware Art Museum
The Storytellers Art: Re-imagining America through Illustration
7 Sept 2011 – Dec 2012
Tales of Folk and Fairies : The Life and work of Katherine Pyle
18 Feb 2012 – 9 Sept 2012
"So Beautifully Illustrated" Katherine Richardson Wireman (1878-1966)
6 Oct 2012 – 6 Jan 2013
Indelible Impressions: Contemporary Illustrators and Howard Pyle
9 Feb 2013 – 1 June 2013
www.delart.org

Art Supplies

londongraphics.co.uk
cowlingandwilcox.com
daler-rowney.com
jacksonsart.com
artsupplies.co.uk
artistmaterial.co.uk

Colleges: Courses in illustration

anglia.ac.uk
arts.brighton.ac.uk
camberwell.arts.ac.uk
ceg-uk.com
coventry.ac.uk
hca.ac.uk
artdesignhull.ac.uk
kingston.ac.uk
nuca.ac.uk
ntu.ac.uk
plymouthart.ac.uk
staffs.ac.uk
aucb.ac.uk
northampton.ac.uk
falmouth.ac.uk
ucreative.ac.uk
uclan.ac.uk
lincoln.ac.uk
camberwell.arts.ac.uk
lcc.arts.ac.uk
wlv.ac.uk
uwic.ac.uk
csm.arts.ac.uk
londonartcollege.co.uk

illustrators Contact Details

mickbrownfield.com
mikebrownlow.com
mylestalbot.com
joannakerr.com
robinedmondsillustration.com
gerryembleton.com
melgrant.com
johnhaslamillustration.com
jonhigham.co.uk
devicefonts.co.uk (Rian Hughes)
johnwatkiss.blogspot.com
stevelavis.com
barrykitson.com
johnwatsonart.com
peter-richardson-illustration.com
notaproperperson.blogspot.com (Peter Doherty)

Shops With illustration Books

bookpalacebooks.com
bookpalace.com
goshlondon.com
page45.com
budsartbooks.com
tate.org.co.uk
marchpane.com

illustration Organisations

theaoi.com
societyillustrators.org
americanartarchives.com
bookillustration.org
illustratorsaustralia.com
associazioneillustratori.it
illustratorsireland.com
bno.nl
lamaisondesillustrateurs.com
io-home.org
apic.es
saahub.com
si-la.org
schoonoverfund.org
rockwell-center.org
rsma.web.co.uk
gava.org.uk
directoryofillustration.com
cepic.org
picture-research.org.uk
pacaoffice.org

illustrators Agents

U.K.
illustrationweb.com
folioart.co.uk
centralillustration.com
debutart.com
arenaillustration.com
theartworksinc.com
inkyillustration.com
organisart.co.uk
artistpartners.com

U.S.
illustrationonline.com

FRANCE
mariebastille.com

If you would like to be listed in our directory please get in touch: 020 8768 0022 (from outside UK: +44 20 8768 0022)
A 4 issue listing plus an expanded annual listing on the website www.illustartorsmag.com is only £85 UK.